THE
Loud Silents

THE
Loud Silents

ORIGINS OF THE SOCIAL PROBLEM FILM

Kay Sloan

UNIVERSITY OF ILLINOIS PRESS
Urbana and Chicago

For William H. Goetzmann,
teacher and friend

© 1988 by the Board of Trustees of the University of Illinois
Manufactured in the United States of America
C 5 4 3 2 1

This book is printed on acid-free paper.

Library of Congress Cataloging-in-Publication Data

Sloan, Kay.
  The loud silents.

  Filmography: p.
  Bibliography: p.
  Includes index.
  1. Social problems in motion pictures. 2. Motion
pictures—History. I. Title.
PN1995.9.S62S58   1988 791.43'09'09355   88-4722
ISBN 0-252-01544-4

Contents

Preface
and Acknowledgments

In 1967, *In the Heat of the Night* and *Hurry Sundown* played the drive-in circuits in Mississippi, where I was growing up. At the time, the momentum of the civil rights movement had already peaked, setting into motion cultural changes that *began,* at least, to address the issue of racial equality. National newspapers, television, and radio had played an important role in those changes, as powerful media images conveyed the struggles of the era. It was a time in which the culture itself seemed on the verge of massive upheavals—upheavals for which the media provided a crucial stage. And, as *In the Heat of the Night* and *Hurry Sundown* proved at Mississippi drive-ins in 1967, fiction films could set their own stage for the problems of the Deep South as well. Such movies turned the deepest social conflicts into entertainment that forced my friends and me to question and challenge the culture around us as we were growing up.

From that early experience in Mississippi came my initial interest in the subject matter of this book. What role does our entertainment play in promoting tolerance for social changes? Why are certain issues acceptable by the media for such public examination? How are they then presented as entertainment? What changes, if any, are promoted? What relationship does entertainment have to the cultural consciousness of mass audiences? And finally, how might entertainment link human desire and discontent with society's need for cultural continuity? These are sweeping questions, to be sure. But in the origins of a new entertainment form—the movies—might lie at least a few clues to these broad issues.

To the extent that narrative centers on conflicts springing from human interaction, virtually all films, of course, deal with "social problems." For the purposes of this book, my interest lay in locating those early films that were *primarily* concerned with societally defined "issues," regardless of their genre—and regardless of whether the film was a message pleading for a specific reform, although many, in fact, were such pleas. In my search for how these early motion pictures delivered social conflicts to the public, I have had the encouragement and help of many people.

Certainly, no scholarly work is created in a vacuum, although time in archives and at the computer is a solitary task. That task was made a less solitary one by a circle of friends, colleagues, and critics who have variously challenged, advised, and encouraged me. William H. Goetzmann provided important critical commentary and intellectual inspiration during the early stages of this book. Similarly, Thomas Schatz, Horace Newcomb, and Robert E. Davis offered many useful criticisms. In other stages of the manuscript, Louis Black, Jackie Byars, Elliott Gorn, Danae Clark, and Paul Finkelman contributed valuable suggestions, editorial comments, or clues that helped me trace the whereabouts of often-elusive motion pictures.

I am also indebted to numerous archivists who helped me locate those motion pictures: Emily Siegal and Cooper C. Graham at the Library of Congress, Audrey Kupfterberg at the American Film Institute, Jan Christopher Horak at the George Eastman House, Anthony Slide at the Motion Picture Academy of Arts and Sciences, Charles Silver at the Museum of Modern Art's Film Study Center, Richard Koszarski at the American Museum of the Moving Image, and archivists at the Pacific Film Archive in Berkeley and the Paul Killiam Motion Picture Collection in New York. Bill Wortman at Miami University's King Library furnished archival material important to this study. My student assistants at Miami University, Ginger Lesh and Theresa Horn, were energetic researchers and typists, and their help greatly facilitated this book.

The American Council of Learned Societies provided a generous grant for much of my research. The McMurray Foundation of Dallas, Texas, also deserves many thanks for its financial support of the chapter on woman suffrage films. I am also grateful to both the University of Texas at Austin for two university fellowships and to

Miami University for several small grants and for an academic leave that allowed me time to complete this book.

Portions of this book, in different form, have appeared in *American Quarterly, Cineaste,* and *Film History.*

K.S.

Université Libre de Bruxelles
Brussels, Belgium

Introduction:
Front Page Movies

Maggie always departed with raised spirits from these melodramas. She rejoiced at the way in which the poor and virtuous
eventually overcame the wealthy and wicked. The theatre
made her think.

—Stephen Crane, *Maggie: A Girl of the Streets*

Sheiks, flappers, comic tramps, and vamps: silent film has left
a legacy of bizarrely colorful images preserved in the popular mind by
nostalgia. Yet in the early days of the primitive film industry, the
cinema treated social problems in a way that was, ironically, as
fantastic as the glamorous stars and tinsel world of Hollywood's later
silver screen. The earliest audiences pushed their coins across box
office windows to watch melodramas and comedies that often celebrated characters who literally animated the social and political
dilemmas of the Progressive Era. The cinema turned these dilemmas
into fairy tales of the day. Greedy corporate tycoons, villainous landlords, corrupt politicians, flamboyant suffragettes, and striking workers
flickered across the bedsheets that sometimes sufficed for screens in
hastily created moviehouses just after the turn of the century.

This is the story of that early silent cinema, a largely precorporate,
inconsistently censored film industry that had its roots not in Hollywood
but in the nation's inner cities. It is an important story both for the
vision it provides of how entertainment can deliver social problems to
the public, and for the historical portrait it paints of America just after
the turn of the century. In the era before World War I, moviegoing
often involved paying a nickel or a dime to watch a series of short one
or two reelers in the cramped quarters of storefront theaters that
populated the urban ghettoes.[1] The elaborate movie "palace" was, for

the most part, an anomaly; so was the feature film. Film companies were small business operations that might shoot several one-reel films every week in a makeshift studio. This was a time when the traditions of the cinema were in the process of formation, when both the subject matter and the form of film were in flux. Inventions rapidly became conventions that helped shore up a sense of social order, as a new art form began to link human desire with the needs of society.

In New York, Chicago, Boston, and in an obscure community called Hollywood out in California, small film companies often turned to the literary and political milieu of the muckrakers and the Progressives for storylines. The "muckraking" cinema cranked out stories that entertained primarily working-class audiences who could afford the five- or ten-cent price of admission to the nickelodeons. There, seated on wooden folding chairs, moviegoers watched graphic portrayals of America's social problems, some of which were part of their everyday lives.

In 1910, Walter Fitch, a film critic for the *Moving Picture World,* one of the film industry's first trade journals, stepped back from the immediacy of the new medium—it was, indeed, a cinema in search of itself—to take a long look at its potential and its possibilities. Filmmakers, mused Fitch, "may play on every pipe in the great organ of humanity."[2] The early cinema did indeed attempt to compose euphonious sounds from the cacophony of the era. With titles such as *Capital Versus Labor, The Suffragettes' Revenge, A Corner in Wheat, The Usurer's Grip, The Girl Strike Leader,* or *The Reform Candidate,* all released in the first fifteen years of the twentieth century, the cinema championed the cause of labor, lobbied against political "bosses," and often gave dignity to the struggles of the urban poor. Conversely, other films satirized suffragists, ridiculed labor organizers, and celebrated America's corporate leaders in antilabor melodramas that the American Federation of Labor denounced and boycotted.

The period itself encompassed vast contradictions. While socialists such as Eugene Debs and Mother Jones fought for drastic changes in the nation's economic system, the new industrial leaders attempted paternalistic, philanthropic solutions to labor activism. At the same time that radicals pushed for fundamental changes in American life, middle-class reformers lobbied for legislation on labor and women's rights that would offer moderate change within the existing structure. Progressive thinkers such as the economist Richard T. Ely and the sociologists Edward A. Ross and Thorstein Veblen condemned what they saw as the dynamics of inequality in America; their voices became part of the milieu of protest in which the movies were born.[3] Others like Louis D. Brandeis, later a Supreme Court justice, indicted the banking system he analyzed in *Other People's Money,* and successfully challenged corporate America in the courts. Muckraking journalists exposed the horrors of child labor and the corruption of political machinery in the nation's magazines and newspapers. Articles by such investigative journalists decried "the shame of the cities" and their failure to adequately meet the needs of their citizens. Upton Sinclair created a national furor by exposing unsanitary meat-packing conditions in his novel *The Jungle;* Frank Norris took on railroad tycoons in *The Octopus.* Lincoln Steffens's articles for *Everybody's Magazine,* with their prostitutes, gamblers, policemen "on the take," corporate tycoons, and greedy landlords, provided an array of stories that pointed to the need for social change.

It was a volatile, exciting world for the new lively entertainment form of the motion picture to enter. Conflicts that challenged the foundations of society found their way into the cinema as film companies seized on the news in the headlines for rich melodramatic and comic material. They also documented contemporary events in early newsreels. In an era long before the advent of television, motion pictures served as news reportage and propaganda at the same time that they revolutionized entertainment. Savvy political figures quickly learned to use the new medium to advertise themselves. In 1906, William Randolph Hearst made talking films of his campaign speeches to circulate in areas in which his personal travel was difficult.[4] Performing a function similar to that of a modern television reporter, the filmmaker Siegmund Lubin released films in 1908 reporting the campaigns of the political rivals William Jennings Bryan and John W. Kern.[5] But, though the films showing news events or national political campaigns served as important justifications for the existence of the often-criticized new medium of the motion picture, the fictions of those actual conflicts told a richer story about the climate of the period. The fictionalization of conflicts allowed an injection of fantasy and ideology into the stories. Films interpreted the nation's headlines in dramatic visual images that at once persuaded and entertained. The comedies, melodramas, and occasional westerns about labor conflict, tenement poverty, or political corruption reveal through fantasy an America torn with ideological conflict.

Often, special interest groups made their own motion pictures in collaboration with film industrialists. An important part of the process of translating the news involved opening the channels of filmmaking to groups advocating change. The earliest film audiences watched motion pictures made or sponsored by groups like the National Child Labor Committee, the National American Woman Suffrage Association, and even by individuals such as Upton Sinclair and the Progressive New York Governor, William Sulzer, who produced and starred in his own melodrama in 1914.[6] Other Progressive activists joined them. For instance, the birth control activist Margaret Sanger made a melodrama to promote the basic civil liberties that she was repeatedly denied during the Progressive Era.[7]

Conservatives as well as Progressives seized on the new medium as a way to dramatize their ideas. Organizations such as the National Association of Manufacturers and the Russell Sage Foundation made film melodramas to promote corporate paternalism. Such films circulated through the nation's moviehouses as if they were no different from slapstick comedies, westerns, and historical dramas. Distributors offered such politically oriented films to exhibitors along with material produced solely for entertainment. Often, a film reviewer would suggest to exhibitors that a motion picture with a prolabor message, for instance, or a plea for women's rights would be popular in areas where such ideas were already accepted.[8] Essentially, the early audiences paid their nickels and dimes to see the political tracts of special interest groups on the same program as less controversial material.

Regardless of the ideological message, however, the vision that commercial film could serve as a vehicle for overt political causes seems startling—even revolutionary—today. For instance, Progressive Era woman suffragists made melodramas in collaboration with Hollywood film companies. Certainly it is difficult to imagine a modern-day equivalent: the National Organization of Women collaborating with Twentieth Century Fox in the early 1980s to make a melodrama starring Meryl Streep or Jane Fonda promoting the Equal Rights Amendment might be such an event. By contemporary standards, such a film would be an utter aberration from Hollywood practices. Yet in the early twentieth century, such was the notion of what film might—and even should—be. Film became a vehicle for overtly presenting social problems to the public.

The rise of the feature length film during the World War I years contributed to the decline of the numerous early social problem films. Since demand for motion pictures dictated that the companies turn out films rapidly, it was crucial that story ideas be readily found. It was easier for filmmakers to take risks about controversial issues in an era when the companies were releasing, as one Hollywood veteran remembers, at least "one reel a week."[9] When film companies turned out several short films a month, the production of a potentially controversial film was far less of an economic risk than it would be in the later age of the blockbuster. Even without the encouragement and participation of special interest groups, the young film companies made melodramas and comedies that exploited the issues splashed across the nation's headlines.

One of the most notorious of these films bore the innocent title of *Why?*. Released in 1913, *Why?* shocked critics with its tale of corrupt elites and its vision of workers revolting against capitalism in America. The film's hero, a fiery-eyed immigrant with wild hair, dreamed of revenge against the wealthy classes who feasted while enslaved workers starved. The three parts of *Why?* contained episodes of capitalists and workers shooting it out with revolvers over child labor, corporate greed, and class inequality. In a scene that could have been scripted by Marx himself, the capitalists turn into sacks of gold when shot. Released by the American arm of the independent French company Eclair Films, *Why?* culminated with workers burning down Manhattan. The blazes, ironically, had been handpainted red by workers for the capitalist film company. The film ended with the Woolworth building still burning, violating one of the ideological tenets of the bourgeois narrative closure that flames, like western bad guys or melodramatic villains, have to die in the end. Instead of restoring responsibility and order, the film simply left its audience in a liminal world that granted power and legitimacy to unleashed desire. "Socialist doctrine!" cried one outraged reviewer.[10]

Why?'s virtual celebration of anarchy frightened censors as well as critics. Early censors feared the political content of films as much as their occasional sexual content. The potential of the cinema to champion such organized violence disturbed Frederic C. Howe, the chairman of the National Board of Censorship of Motion Pictures. That organization had been formed by the filmmakers themselves in 1909 to discourage "immoral" or "lurid" material that had roused criticism from more traditional sectors of society. Howe feared the mounting success of radical, politically oriented moving pictures. He was a liberal reformer, but hardly a radical. Despite local outcries over the supposed "immorality" of the movies, Howe suggested that the political role of film was potentially as threatening to society as were its challenges to a Victorian moral code.[11]

Particularly since the early films touched the sentiments of masses of people, including the millions of newly arrived immigrants to whom the English printed word was still a mystery, they elicited condemnation from those, like Howe, who feared the power of the motion picture over those in the ghetto.[12] Motion pictures, noted one journalist in 1908, had become "both a clubhouse and an academy for the workingman."[13] The class of people attending motion pictures, stated another observer delicately, "are not of the rich."[14] At their outset, motion pictures found audiences primarily among the many Americans whose lives were dominated by the uncertainties of poverty and the cultural ruptures of immigration.

Thus Frederic Howe worried about the content of films in 1914. The films that "tended to excite class feeling or . . . tend to bring discredit upon the agencies of the government," wrote Howe, could lead to a time "when the movie . . . becomes the daily press of industrial groups, of classes, of Socialism, syndicalism, and radical opinion."[15]

Howe's fears, of course, remained unfounded. The revolutionary content of *Why?* was an anomaly among the early social problem films. The young film companies themselves attempted to make their business more "respectable," and broaden the appeal of motion pictures to the middle classes. They made the social problem films as part of that process, with the notion that such films might be seen as "educational" and "uplifting."

It was a cinematic role encouraged by critics. In 1913, one film journalist suggested that the cinema might be a weapon "in the battle against child labor, white-slavery, labor-conflicts, and vice development."[16] He suggested that film should take up the subjects headlined on the front pages of the nation's newspapers and "expose injustice, cruelty, and suffering in all their naked ugliness."[17] This critic suggested that both the film industry's need for stories and America's pressing social problems might be settled if only the filmmakers would turn their attention to social issues. But the solution to such issues, he emphasized, must be calm, reasoned change, not the revolutionary message of a film like *Why?*

Such liberal film critics played an important role in channeling film into a vehicle for middle-class reforms. They pointed out causes that might be taken up in melodrama and applauded those films that did crusade.[18] The *Moving Picture World*'s Louis Reeves Harrison promoted the role that film could play in pointing out the need for social reform, and he denounced what he called "the desire for power on the part of the ruling classes." Filmmakers, he urged, should pay attention to such inequities in corporate society.[19] The cinema might act as a cultural watchdog, appealing for responsibility from all levels of society. One issue demanding treatment by the moving pictures, suggested Harrison, was child labor—another was what he applauded as women's "broadening knowledge and experience." The expression of those issues could not only strengthen the nation, but the role of film in it.

In 1912, Harrison reminded filmmakers that the often-denigrated cinema might serve as a tool for "uplifting" the masses. He offered a virtual litany of themes for the melodrama that expressed the interests of both the era's reformers and some early filmmakers:

> the social battle for justice to those who do the world's work, the adjustment of compensation to labor, the right of common people to liberty and the pursuit of happiness, the betterment of humanity through the prevention of crime rather than its cure, the prevention of infant mortality, and the prevention of hoggishness wherever theatrical trusts will permit, the self-conflict between material tendency and spiritual clarification, all these furnish subjects of widespread interest which the dramatist may handle with or without gloves.[20]

The film industry increasingly addressed the issues suggested by Harrison. In 1914, one film director boasted that he got the "best points for [his] work from the newspapers," turning the turmoil of the era into comedy and melodrama.[21]

Concerned that the cinema raised subversive questions, Howe neglected the important role it played in laying them to rest. *Why?*'s radical solution to class conflict was, not surprisingly, rare in the cinema. It represented the starkest challenge to the nation's economic powers—the wheat speculators, tenement owners, loan sharks, or captains of industry. More typically, the films dealt with social problems in a way that muted their critiques of economic or social injustice. They called for careful reforms or fatalistic surrenders to uncontrollable "natural" forces that doled out troubles and misfortunes. Such films proved that the radically new entertainment form of the cinema could act as a conservative force in the emerging industrial society.

For instance, the Thomas Edison Company's *The Usurer's Grip* was a modern-day fairy tale set in the tenements. Funded by the Russell Sage Foundation in 1912, the film warned audiences about unscrupulous money lenders who thrived on the poverty stricken, hounding them further and further into financial desperation. The film's hero and heroine found themselves in mounting debt to a usurer, but they were saved at last by an understanding businessman who directed them to the loan division of the Russell Sage Foundation. There they were rescued by the paternalism promoted by Sage's vision of benevolent capitalism.[22] *The Usurer's Grip* was a self-serving advertisement for the Sage Foundation. Such early films precursed modern television advertising by blending entertainment with commercial messages. Through melodrama, the Edison Company and the Russell Sage Foundation advertised direct social reform and suggested that philanthropic measures might remedy urban poverty.

Increasingly, the early films moved from primitive one or two reelers exploiting class conflict to more sophisticated films with complicated plots. At times, they advocated specific reforms. Film began to shift from the sensationalism of muckraking issues into serious calls for reform through "enlightenment"—whether it be better management to assuage striking workers, calls for woman suffrage, the abolition of child labor, poor tenement conditions, and the illegality of birth control. Film industrialists tried to establish the middle-class nature of the cinema by allowing reform groups or special interest groups access to the medium. In 1912, the National Association of Manufacturers (NAM) collaborated with Thomas Edison's Company to make a propagandistic melodrama on factory safety called *The Crime of Carelessness.* It was written by the Progressive writer James Oppenheim, who was quickly earning a reputation as a writer of what the *New York Times* called "social films."[23] His first film for the Edison Company, titled *Hope,* had dealt with the problem of tuberculosis. With *The Crime of Carelessness,* he turned to the more controversial issue of problems in the workplace. The film laid equal blame for hazardous working conditions on workers and negligent owners—but insidiously punished a careless worker for a factory fire.[24] The problems of the workplace, then, might be resolved merely by responsibility on the part of individual employees. It was, wrote the *New York Times* critic, a "long and stirring drama," one of a line of Oppenheim's "social films."[25] NAM's film, of course, did more than link industrial problems with careless workers. It also linked the interests of the film industry with those of the larger corporate interests represented by NAM.

A similar theme emerged in the Vitagraph Company's *Capital Versus Labor,* an exposé of labor problems made in 1910. Punctuated by bloody scenes of rioting workers battling company-hired thugs, the film suggested that the strikers had legitimate grievances to air. But the workers alone were powerless to change their situation. The eventual "happy ending" came not through the organized protests or negotiations of labor unions, but through the intervention of the church. The violence in *Capital Versus Labor* continued until a minister finally calmed the mobs and convinced the greedy capitalist to compromise with his workers.[26] The film thus revealed the futility of rioting in the streets while it still acknowledged the validity of the strikers' complaints. From such plots came a dual statement about workers in America: while the films granted them dignity and self-worth as individuals, it also rendered them and their organizations powerless. *The Crime of Carelessness* and *Capital Versus Labor* serve as examples of how workers might be portrayed as irresponsible individuals who are ultimately dependent on the good graces of their generous bosses.

Such films relied on the "happy ending," which provided audiences with continuity and faith in "the system." Even actual historical events were rewritten to accommodate that expectation. A 1915 melodrama on political corruption in New York City provides a telling example of how important the happy ending had become. *The Governor's Boss* took a political tragedy and transformed it into victory for the democratic process. The film was one of the most unusual melodramas made about political corruption for another reason: it actually starred an impeached governor of New York, William Sulzer.

Sulzer publicized his case against the Tammany Hall machine in 1915 with a melodrama written by James S. Barcus, a friend and political crony. He first took it to Broadway, where the play had a brief run of sixteen performances at the Garrick Theatre.[27] Following the play's unsuccessful Broadway run, he turned to the cinema with the script. To heighten the realism of the film, Sulzer played himself in the starring role, but he took the unique opportunity that film provided to rewrite his own history with a happy ending. *The Governor's Boss* ended not with Sulzer's impeachment, but with the defeat of his opponents in court. Sulzer restored justice and democracy to New York City through the power of the cinema rather than the power of political office. Imagine Richard Nixon producing and starring in a cinematic version of Watergate in 1975 — with an ending in which he retained his grip on the presidency. Despite the vast differences between Sulzer and Nixon, the preposterous nature of the contemporary example is nevertheless a striking indication of just how unique this Progressive Era vision of film as political propaganda was.

Like the many previous melodramas calling for social change, *The Governor's Boss* restored democracy in such a way that rendered the film a less powerful statement against Tammany Hall. The *New York Times* critic found the ending so absurd that he sarcastically observed that "the Governor, his secretary, his daughter, and Virtue in general triumph."[28] Even real occurrences took on fantastic proportions to assure a society in distress that its institutions worked for the good of all, despite the news broadcast in the nation's headlines.

The headlines were powerful material in a time when muckraking journalists and novelists like Ida Tarbell and Upton Sinclair constantly probed the underside of the "American Dream." Both Sinclair and Tarbell were among the era's crusaders who made their own films. Their cinematic efforts reflected a period in film history when the motion pictures were seen as a medium that might be open to the public, particularly to those with a cause. Tarbell, who had condemned John D. Rockefeller when she exposed the ruthless practices of the Standard Oil Company in 1902, collaborated with Vitagraph Studios in 1914 as part of their series of photoplays scripted by "famous authors."[29] Interestingly, she chose not a political subject but a historical play to dramatize, as part of a broader effort by the membership of the Authors' League of America to help less recognized writers. In 1913, Upton Sinclair ambitiously put his powerful exposé of the meat-packing industry, *The Jungle,* into five reels of a motion picture.[30] At the same time, however, the issues that Tarbell and

Sinclair were publicizing with their news articles and novels found their way into the cinema in ways that were less overtly political than *The Jungle*. Motion pictures took on the preoccupations of muckraking journalists and absorbed them into the ethos of individualism and the "virtue" that mended society in *The Governor's Boss*. In that process, they helped establish film as a respectable entertainment form, as they mediated the problems of society.

Many security-minded reformers from the educated middle class saw that new function of film and moved from their early position of unrelenting condemnation of the newly emerged entertainment form to an attempt to "re-form" it. These reformers realized that film had the capacity to solve problems, to suggest solutions that would contain disorder and push forward moderate change. Their motion pictures raised issues among masses of people that the printed word might not reach, as Walter Fitch had commented in 1910. Film critics such as Louis Reeves Harrison and his colleagues at the *Moving Picture World*, W. Stephen Bush and the Reverend E. Boudinot Stockton, all had long stressed the use of film to "uplift." Jane Addams turned from her call for censorship of the moving pictures ("debased" and "primitive" she had called them in 1909)[31] to actually starring in a melodrama in 1913 titled *Votes for Women*. Filmmaking seemed to have become fashionable among liberal reformers.

In their collaboration with professional filmmakers, the reformers used some of the conventions rapidly developing in the film to serve their own purposes. Through the "happy ending," the films presented the possibility that change could take place without massive upheaval or disruption. Such purposes led reformers such as Jane Addams to move from initial condemnation of the motion picture to praise for its capacity to "uplift" or "educate." Film could serve the interests of the middle class and of the film industry by appealing to a broader audience by using virtuous calls for reform.

The reformist dramas provided a respectable mission for a cinema in search of itself. By 1915, the poet and film critic Vachel Lindsay could observe that "the motion picture goes almost as far as journalism into the social fabric in some ways, further in others."[32] Whatever their political message, however, films penetrated the social fabric even further than did muckraking journalists by tapping fantasy as well as reality, animating and heightening the stories told in print. The cinema offered fantastic solutions that appealed to unconscious human desire at the same time that it raised problems of everyday life.

Some of this process had been observed as early as 1915 during the height of the early silent film era. In the summer of that year, a portly, balding psychologist from Harvard discovered a diversion from Boston's humid afternoons. Professor Hugo Munsterberg became one of the cinema's most ardent devotees. Munsterberg's first movie experience, a somewhat risqué film called *Neptune's Daughter,* had been, by his own daughter's account, one of the most startling adventures of the professor's life.[33] Settled in the anonymous darkness of a theater, he had watched a fascinating phenomenon unfold. On the movie screen before him, the actress Annette Kellerman danced in a costume that left little to the imagination. But what fascinated the professor even more than Kellerman were the actual illustrations of the nuances of human perception that he had studied and taught for years in the university. Munsterberg was captivated by the manner in which the camera appeared to virtually become the human eye, and in which it might also create a new vision of the world controlled by moral forces. He spent the rest of the summer of 1915 carefully studying the new art form, even securing for himself a personal tour of the Vitagraph Studios.

Part of Munsterberg's interest lay in interpreting how the cinema dwelled on human needs and how it could direct the emotions of audiences. In a treatise on the motion picture, *The Photoplay,* published by the psychologist shortly before he died in 1916, he laid the foundation for a sophisticated theory of film. One of the greatest attractions of the cinema, he suggested, was its "stirring up of desires together with their constant fulfillment."[34]

More than a simple mirroring of visual perception, motion pictures became immensely popular with the masses in those formative years because, in part, they captured the enduring subtleties of human desire, with their tales of wistful longing for a better life. "The work of art," explained Munsterberg, "aims to keep both the demand and its fulfillment forever awake."[35] The theater thus roused longing while it also left audiences with the "constant fulfillment" recognized by the psychologist. The popular culture emerging at the turn of the century acted as an agent of both social cohesion and the desire for change. That process emerges as the protest films addressed political and social subjects that held the capacity to rupture society.

Entertainment in itself involves a certain rupturing—a temporary suspension of belief in the outside world takes place along with a suspension of disbelief in the inner world constructed through entertainment. The melodrama of social protest suspended audiences between what they escaped *from* (their everyday lives) and what they escaped *to* (a more romantic version of the situation that structured those daily lives). By often resolving those situations in "happily ever after" endings, movies released their audiences from the grim cinematic creations of shabby tenement life, or sweatshop lines, into a world transformed, however briefly, into a realm where fantasy entered the tenement or sweatshop on the wings of romance or sudden wealth. If the melodramas refused to allow such interventions, they at least endowed their heroes and heroines with dignity.

A whole host of archetypal villains and victims danced in the flickering lights of the nickelodeons in a melodramatic exorcism of social wrongs. Such archetypes have never really left the motion picture—nor has the "happy ending," which restored faith in the enduring individual. In its early era of inventions, the cinema also set conventions. The primitive social problem films were the beginning of a long psychological trip into the present with which they are intimately joined.[36] Like any pioneers, the early movies were original, but the trail they blazed into the American psyche became a familiar path marked with desires and frustrations—and so timeworn that we have taken its twists and turns for granted.

By the eve of World War I, most of the small film companies were gone, and with them the storefront nickelodeons and those primitive short films that raised social problems, much as the muckrakers did. Those formative years of the cinema, unique as they were, established the manner in which films continue to raise social issues while at the same time containing them in satisfactory bourgeois resolutions. America's dilemmas are in many ways similar to those faced by the country just after the turn of the century—overcrowding, sexual inequalities, political corruption, and corporate irresponsibility still find their way into a cinema that solves those problems in a private fashion, just as the early films did. But never again will the process be quite so blatant as in the silent social problem films.

Something was forgotten in the following decades, or lost in sentimentalized versions of the early period. In 1915, Vachel Lindsay expressed a thought that is poignant in retrospect. He dramatically claimed that film is a "new weapon of men, and the face of the whole earth changes."[37] Lindsay, regrettably, was wrong. Much still remains to be explored and "remembered" from that era when "the whole earth changed" because of a new entertainment form.

In those one or two reelers are more than the origins of the social problem film. The films contain cultural signposts of paramount importance about how entertainment shapes the political issues affecting the lives of moviegoers. They are a reminder of the capacity of film to explore the problems of society and lessen their threat while still suggesting the need for change. When Stephen Crane's fictional Maggie attended her turn-of-the-century melodramas, she would leave "with raised spirits" after watching people like herself defeat those with power over them. Though such triumphs in the cinema were measured in terms of religious redemptions or acts of fate, they were still significant glimpses into class conflict in America. Within that complex role is buried an even deeper significance. The films also reveal a society struggling to maintain order in a period of terrific unrest—an order that allowed inequality and the essential powerlessness of the average American to continue.

Those days when the film industry was young reveal that the cinema reverberates through time itself. It goes beyond its specific era to illuminate the ongoing power of the motion picture to dramatize the needs and desires of its viewers through generations of archetypal characters and situations. Like H. G. Wells's heroes, one can travel into the past with the flick of a switch on a projection machine and discover America at the turn of the century. Unfortunately, however, such a cinematic "journey" can be as difficult as a ride on Wells's time machine: many of the films simply no longer exist, and can be known only through reviews or synopses. When silent films lost their commercial viability within several years after release, the film companies, eager for fast production and quick profits, carelessly discarded them. Often the companies themselves were too short-lived to maintain their films. The perishable silver nitrate stock on which the motion pictures were printed further reduced their chance for survival. As early as 1906, one critic recognized the danger of losing such valuable cultural artifacts as the new motion picture. "We often wonder where all the films that are made and used a few times go to," he wrote, "and the questions come up in our minds, again and again: Are the manufacturers aware that they are making history? Do they realize that in fifty or one hundred years the films now being made will be curiosities?"[38] Now, some eighty years later, one only wishes that filmmakers had listened to his admonition. The films that exist today are rare cultural documents.

Though the preserved film footage offers valuable insight into the climate of American cultural and political tensions, an understanding of their full impact must, ironically, rely heavily on original printed material. Controversy over the issues of social protest spilled over into the pages of early trade magazines such as the *Moving Picture World*, *Motography*, *Variety*, and *Photoplay*. Their reviews testify to the lively arguments over workers' rights, class conflict, political graft, and sexual politics that the films once delivered.

Such themes that the films repeatedly explored illustrate the larger dilemmas of society in dealing with injustices and inequalities. For that reason, the following chapters are not chronological but thematic. The first issue-oriented chapter explores the class-bound nature of early melodrama and what the sociologist Edward A. Ross called "criminaloids"—those who grew wealthy by exploiting the poor. Such characters made ideal villains in films that ventured into the inner circles of the nation's corrupt elites. Chapter two delves into the "cinema of the submerged," particularly as D. W. Griffith defined it. There, a cinema made heroes and heroines out of those "submerged" in powerlessness. Tenement dwellers attempted to flee the ghetto, and escaped prisoners tried to elude their captors in plots that pointed out the plight of the victims of economic or legal injustice.

In the labor union films discussed in chapter three, working-class heroes fought back against their employers. But the problem of "Capital Versus Labor," as the film of that title designated it, varied from visions of unruly "ferret-eyed workers" to cruel "fat cat" factory owners who exploited children and honest working people. White slavery, a subject of the next chapter on sexual politics, was one of the most controversial topics ever sensationalized by the cinema. Taken alone, it was a euphemism for forced prostitution. The central concern of the explosive white slavery films and the melodramas on alcoholism and birth control was the preservation of the private sphere of the family.

The films about the woman suffrage movement, the subject of the last chapter, brought together a wide spectrum of propaganda for and against the movement. Caricatures of man-hating suffragettes paraded across movie screens as comedies ridiculed the notion of women voting. Suffragists themselves fought back with movie cameras, countering the comic attack with persuasive melodramas starring beautiful suffragist heroines. They elevated film into a significant political tool for their cause. The suffrage films, with their span of satire, newsreels, and melodramas, offer an opportunity to look at the tremendous range of political positions that the cinema took on a single subject.

The early risk-taking silent filmmakers saw their new medium as one that could both entertain and, in due course, instruct. They catered to the masses with a gamut of social commentary that reflected the traditional American belief that once social wrongs were exposed to the people, the people would see to it that they were righted. More importantly, the companies catered to the masses to build their own business empires. Thus they were reformers who also sought a profit; with their sermons on social injustice and their faith in the individual, they became, quite unintentionally, America's newest street preachers, making movies that became indeed "loud silents."

CHAPTER 1

Celluloid Criminaloids

Wine distilled from the blood of unfortunates —
Viands paid for with the tears of the needy.
— *The Usurer*, 1910

In the summer of 1910, a melodrama called *The Usurer* featured a money lender who, according to a title card, "lived high on monies gleaned from others." It was part of an entire series of films that exposed not only greed but the clash of economic classes, and the domination of the poor by what they portrayed as a corrupt, power-mad few. The sociologist Edward A. Ross had coined a term in 1907 — *criminaloids* — for those, like the usurer, who exploited their positions of power for personal gain.[1] The descriptions of corporate greed and political corruption he offered in his book *Sin and Society* demonstrated the indifference of those in power to the needs of the poor. But in the motion pictures of the day, his ideas found a more primitive expression. The villains of films like *The Usurer, A Corner in Wheat,* and *A Legal Hold-Up* were the nation's robber barons, money lenders, and corrupt policemen and politicians. The film industry took Ross's "criminaloids" and cast them in roles that sometimes portrayed the class system in America as brutal and exploitative.

A Legal Hold-Up, The Coal Heavers, The Nihilist, The Subpoena Server, The Kleptomaniac—films like these inspired one critic to throw up his hands in despair over the apparently radical nature of the new cinema. In 1906, a writer for *The Christian Leader* predicted that "a set of revolutionists training for the overthrow of the government could find no surer means than these exhibitions."[2] In *The Subpoena Server,* a satire of John D. Rockefeller, audiences of 1906 could watch one of America's most important capitalists stripped of his economic power. After the Standard Oil Company collided with the government over the questionable reaches of its monopoly, the cinema proved that even the president of that powerful company was not immune from cinematic barbs. *The Subpoena Server* capitalized on Ida Tarbell's exposé of Standard Oil in *McClure's Magazine,* the journal that helped spawn the muckraking era. The bulletin accompanying the film explained that its short scenario "followed the recent experience of the Standard Oil Magnate."³ A title card informed viewers that here was "the American millionaire in his amusing pastime of dodging papers." Like the screwball comedies of the depression, this early farce showed the wealthy class as wacky and eccentric. Such satires reduced Rockefeller's abuse of corporate control to mere "antics" or "amusing pastimes" that gave the public the right to laugh at the rich—and thus gave the ordinary moviegoer a certain sense of power.

The year 1906 was also one in which Edwin S. Porter directed *The Kleptomaniac,* a film that cast an even greater negative light on those in power in America. Along with *The Subpoena Server,* the film could have provided the incentive for the *Christian Century* journalist's indictment of motion pictures. *The Kleptomaniac* offered a scathing portrait of the American legal system and its treatment of the poor. Its heroine, a penniless woman of the tenements, stole a loaf of bread to feed her daughter, and was sentenced to jail. A parallel story within the plot revealed a wealthy woman acquitted for shoplifting luxury items from a department store. Court scenes when the two are brought to trial resembled a virtual assembly line of justice—as marshalls herded the accused before the judge like so many cattle. Yet the wealthy were brushed out of the courtroom with a sympathetic wave of the hand. One privileged woman clicked her heels in delight as the judge dismissed her case.

The nation's "criminaloids," suggested Porter's film, stretched even to those in judicial robes who dictated the lives of the poor—a message left unmistakable in the final scenes of the film. The female figure of Justice appeared, precariously balancing gold and bread in her scales; slowly the weight slipped to the sack of gold. The blindfold fell from Justice's eyes and she, too, greedily eyed the wealth. Even the legal system, according to *The Kleptomaniac,* rested on economic interests. Significantly, the poor remained powerless in the film. Though *The Kleptomaniac* criticized the injustices of the American legal system, it also informed audiences that they had no real power to correct those injustices. A similar film, *The Scales of Justice,* told virtually the same story in 1906. This time, the poor woman stole shoes for her barefooted children, but the ending was the same.[4]

Other films allowed audiences to watch the transformation of those in power, who changed through either an act of fate or a nagging conscience. But, despite the concern of the *Christian Leader*'s critic, rarely were the villains changed because those they exploited actually challenged them. The message implied that the powerless in America, like the protagonists of *The Kleptomaniac* and *The Scales of Justice*, would remain passive victims of greed and injustice. Yet such messages challenged the status quo in a way that made even Progressive reformers like Jane Addams or Frederic Howe uncomfortable; the new film industry, it appeared, catered to the desires of those wishing to drastically alter power in America—in ways feared by those who saw a new entertainment form disseminating often undisguised political messages.

Part of the alarm raised by the cinema was the very newness of the medium. In 1908, a journalist writing for *The Independent* observed the power of moving pictures in the lives of the discontented, the poor, the new Americans. "The effect of this new form of pictorial drama on the public," proclaimed G. E. Walsh, "is without parallel in modern history. . . . In the poorer sections of the cities where innumerable foreigners congregate, the so-called 'nickelodeon' has held preeminent sway for the last year."[5] No effective national censorship existed as Walsh penned his observations in 1908. As he wrote, alarm mounted about what the consequences might be if no rigorous censorship existed. Within only a few months, the National Board of Review was formed to filter out those motion pictures deemed offensive to the public. But even that censorship concerned primarily sexual or moral issues rather than the political controversy feared by Walsh. In storefront theaters, or even in tenements that sometimes held moviehouses, the new Americans living in "the poorer sections" of urban areas watched film programs that included those pointing out inequality in America—as *The Kleptomaniac* did.

Criticisms of the legal system also extended to the police, where corruption went hand in hand with the unjust legal system that Porter exposed. At the time, graft within the nation's urban police departments was so widespread that the New York police commissioner himself could write in 1901 that "the police are practically above the law. Yet in these three years instances have been frequent of policemen in flagrant criminal acts."[6] *Harper's Weekly* could make the sweeping assertion that "in the two largest cities at least the police are in partnership with the criminal classes."[7] Countless critics laid blame for urban vice squarely at the door of the police station. In the midst of the controversy, the social problem film raised the issue of police dishonesty within the nation's cities. With *How They Rob Men in Chicago* and *A Legal Hold-Up* in 1902, filmmakers frowned on the ethics—or the lack of them—in the police force.[8] But in these cases, the critique was done in the context of comedy. The "stars" of these brief scenarios (which were among the first films to tell a narrative story rather than simply show indiscriminate movement or action) were policemen who deliberately stole from innocent citizens. Thus, the early films joined the muckrakers' critique of the police, maintaining that they were often a subversive force in society rather than a means of upholding the law.

That cinematic subversion of authority brought criticism of the films. In Montreal, a community refused to grant a license for a motion picture theater in 1911, largely because of such content. The *Montreal Star* applauded the decision, announcing that in "nine films out of ten, the [story] centers around the mishaps or the maltreatment of a policeman."[9] Along with their mockery of the police, however, the films emphasized the powerlessness of the individual. They exposed the underside of Horatio Alger's optimistic vision of success in America. Corruption, in those early films, continued to disrupt or destroy the lives of the poor.

Such films serve as cultural signifiers, as representations of that larger web of social cohesion and conflict that constructs human life. They are neither mirrors nor windows, but indications of how political and social concerns are negotiated in a private fashion. Their role in that process is, obviously, a complex one. The early cinema vilified those in power in a way that both justified and softened a harsh reality for working-class audiences. Anger at the elites, the leisure class, and the institutions they represented was validated but transformed into something to be endured or cautiously channeled into reform, thus giving an appeasing message to the new middle-class moviegoers. The cultural web—a network of communication that contradicts, converges, and mystifies—could embrace and transform the very elements that threatened it, finally turning the shocking into a cliché, into yet another dramatic convention.

D. W. Griffith's *A Corner in Wheat* demonstrates the process in which a single film might raise issues threatening to society and transform them into "Americanism," what Griffith called "making the world safe for democracy."[10] Three years after Porter directed *The Kleptomaniac, A Corner in Wheat* captured a dramatic public issue—speculation in the wheat market—and delivered a cinematic argument on economic inequality. The film warned of the consequences that wealth and its companion, greed, could bring if one did actually "succeed" in society. In this, one of his most powerful early films, Griffith borrowed from the naturalist literature and the sensational news of the era with his classic tale of corporate greed. Taken from incidents in Frank Norris's short story "A Deal in Wheat" and his novel *The Octopus,* published in 1901, the film condensed those messages into a sweeping one-reel statement on the irresponsibility of wheat speculators. When Biograph Studios released *A Corner in Wheat* in 1909, newspaper headlines were already condemning the profiteering in wheat that economically doomed the growers and consumers. Griffith took the controversy and turned it into entertainment that also informed mass audiences who, perhaps, had neither the time nor the education to read novels or newspapers. The resulting cinematic version of the wheat speculation interpreted the conflict as an offense to the individual—which could be resolved in the private sphere.

A Corner in Wheat was a poetic argument against the era's economic tycoons. It was also a celebration of the simple life of ordinary men and women. Griffith refrained from the sort of revolutionary diatribe present in the Eclair Company's *Why?*. Instead, he captured a vision of America that contrasted the luxurious lives led by the wealthy with those of the vast majority of the nation. Two years before he made *A Corner in Wheat,* Griffith had condemned what he called "the crimes of the greatest men of the day who obtain money by trickery and watered stocks, and other base and ignoble schemes."[11]

As Edwin S. Porter had done in *The Kleptomaniac,* Griffith put parallel editing to effective use in uncovering what his film called the "ignoble schemes" of those in power. Viewers saw the wealthy class in *A Corner in Wheat* feasting on a sumptuous meal; the camera then transported the audience across time and space to watch the poor, forced into destitution by the speculations in the wheat market, standing in bread lines. Opening with a scene reminiscent of Jean

Francois Millet's famous painting *The Gleaners,* the film raised the stature of the simple life to a romantic pedestal while it condemned the selfish destruction wrought by the wheat speculators.

The greed of the economic elite, however, led to their own demise in both Norris's and Griffith's tales. *A Corner in Wheat* ended with the speculator showing his friend through his granary. But his moment of glory was short-lived. While the workers rose to destroy the upper classes in *Why?,* in Griffith's film it was the grain itself—the fruit of the speculator's own greed—that killed the wheat king. The elegant tycoon unceremoniously fell through a shaft in the granary. Wheat, unleashed by the sudden movement, poured down upon him, burying him in his own bonanza.

The doomed wheat king of Griffith's film is Frank Norris's character in *The Octopus,* S. Behrman, who is also swallowed up by his own wheat. The sense of the powerlessness of the ordinary American is also clear in the novel. The hero of *The Octopus* gives a stirring speech that expressed the desperation of working people at the turn of the century. "They own us, these taskmasters of ours; they own our business, they own our legislatures. We cannot escape from them; there is no redress. We are told we can defeat them by the ballot-box; they own the ballot-box. We are told that we must look to the courts for redress; they own the courts . . . And this is America."[12]

Biograph Studio's promotional bulletin on *A Corner in Wheat* boasted of the patience—not the power—of the speculator's victims. "There is no vengeance possible here," announced the studio, "but the hand of God . . . one of the sins that cried to heaven for vengeance is denying food to the hungry."[13] Thus any real resolution to the serious issue was left to divine forces, and the poor needed only to wait for the intervention of the Almighty to sweep away the evils of corporate greed. Like Frank Norris before him, Griffith elected Nature, not human decisions, to lead to social change. The sowers complacently plant their wheat in the final scene, content with the pleasures of the rural life. Such romantic portrayals of agrarianism against the claustrophobic, grim world of the city championed the simple "good" life while America rapidly industrialized.

Endurance, for Griffith as well as for Norris, was the hope of the human race. As Norris's novel concluded, "greed, cruelty, selfishness, and inhumanity are short-lived; the individual suffers, but the race goes on."[14] In the cinema, the hero or heroine of the social problem film suffered, but the film went on to a closure that allowed the social cohesion necessary for society to go on. Griffith's films, epitomized by *A Corner in Wheat,* adopted the fatalistic view of the naturalists. The Kentuckian turned protest into passivity; in the broad spectrum spanning individual endurance, reform, and revolution, he celebrated the lone survivor who endured. Working at Biograph, Griffith often romanticized poverty, emphasizing the gulf between a corrupt monied class and the long-suffering poor. In Griffith's world, hope existed in America, though, and his films turned it into a poetry of perseverance.

A Corner in Wheat transformed Norris's attempt at "The Great American Novel" into powerful visual entertainment that reinforced individualism and faith in the common people. Critics hailed its portrayal of the unfairness of wheat speculation as a monumental achievement in the then-brief history of film. Perhaps no other film since Edwin S. Porter's *The Great Train Robbery* in 1903 could boast of such praise. Journalists from *The Bioscope, The Moving Picture World,* and the *New York Dramatic Mirror* unanimously applauded Griffith's tribute to the survival of the "common people" against unscrupulous speculators.

Biograph, thought the *Dramatic Mirror*'s film critic, had taken a "daring step" into the problems faced in the country. The film was a measure of the "force and power of motion pictures as a means of conveying drama." The *Bioscope* reviewer hailed the film for the "educational and emotional" lesson it taught, while still another journalist suggested that *A Corner in Wheat* "should serve as a warning to those who undertake to corner and control the food supply and an encouragement to those who see the menace in such illegal and altogether inhuman operations."[15] Artistically and politically, the film created a moving canvas, an animated mural of the people, which lifted the struggles of common men and women into more than entertainment. While journalists could make sweeping declarations that "there is not a reader of these lines in America but may have suffered some injury to the gamblers in the Chicago wheat market,"[16] the cinematic portrait that Griffith painted of weary faces brought that injury directly before his viewers. As the Russian director Sergei Eisenstein learned later in the Soviet Union, film was a potent political weapon to express the needs of the masses: no printed word could match either the despair written on the faces of those standing in Griffith's breadlines, or the stark contrast between the classes as the camera jarred the human eye with images that, in rapid succession, compared their plights. After watching Griffith's film, *The Moving Picture World* columnist was inspired to denounce the "terrible practice of cornering commodities that are the necessities of life."[17]

The attempt to capture a possible economic reality like that of the wheat crisis and then represent it with a single individual was an important—and successful—element of the social problem film. The cinema might reduce even a massive economic problem such as cornering the wheat market to a personal question of greed. The accolades won by Griffith in 1908 indicated that the nation's headlines could successfully become cinematic entertainment in the process. Under the guise of realism, films such as *A Corner in Wheat* suggested that such crises could be managed by romance, personal redemption, or the intervention of fate—unreal solutions acted out by voiceless characters moving in a black and white world. Griffith's appeal in *A Corner in Wheat* was to the visceral, to the emotional catharsis that blended outrage over a real economic problem with the satisfaction of a fictional solution.

This was the intersection between reality and fantasy, between conscious need and unconscious desire, at which the early social problem film arrived and began to thrive. Such films served as translators of front-page news at the same time they offered solutions; the front page merged with the fairy tale in a powerful union of the "real world" with fictional transformations of it. In such films, historical forces became subordinate to the capacity of the individual to prevail in a personal sense. And in the process, then, the individual by implication was outside those historical forces, no longer an agent—a subject—of change but an object of endurance.

In an age when film genres were in a formative stage, "inventions" like those Griffith created when he merged realism with fantastic solutions soon became "conventions." Ironically enough, films that challenged greed and profiteering were quickly snatched up and marketed for popular consumption by filmmakers, themselves in search of profits. Even four years after the sensational release of *A Corner in Wheat*, Powers Films produced *His Ideal of Power* to explore commodity speculation. Martin Steel, the film's protagonist, dominated the wheat market until his power threatened to financially ruin the father of his fiancée. Steel surrendered his own "corner in wheat" for another "ideal of power"—one that recognized others.

"For the first time in his life," read the story of the film, "he had come face to face with the needs of others, and he had sacrificed himself."[18] Like many of Griffith's heroes, Steel was awakened by impending romantic disaster, not by a social consciousness of the larger ramifications of his greed. His metamorphosis into a sympathetic hero was complete by the end of the melodrama, with its political and economic issues settled in the context of romance. Such closures softened the edge of biting social commentary.

The film industry's need to turn a quick profit, then, ironically fueled a series of films on capitalism and the greedy personality it fostered. As businessmen or artists involved in a greedy business themselves, filmmakers made motion pictures that shook a melodramatic fist at the avarice of robber barons, landlords, stock speculators, or corrupt politicians, painting caricatures of capitalists. Those caricatures perfectly fit the model described by Edward A. Ross as "criminals of greed."[19] The Chicago theorist's widely read *Sin and Society* mirrored the discontent that sometimes emanated from movie screens. In the book's introduction, Theodore Roosevelt himself praised Ross's condemnation of "the modern high-powered dealer of woe [who] wears immaculate linen, carries a silk hat and a lighted cigar, [and] sins with a calm countenance and a serene soul."[20]

Roosevelt might have been describing the archetypal villain of many a melodrama. That image described the star of both Griffith's *The Usurer* or *A Corner in Wheat,* so similar were the personas of the archetypal greedy capitalist. Obese, cigar puffing, and sporting a top hat, the "usurer" abused his clients with a perfectly "serene" soul. Made in 1910, the film opens with a scene of the money lender feasting on food and wine. A title card soon informs the audience that the wine is "distilled from the blood of unfortunates" and his "viands [are] paid for with the tears of the needy." The usurer, "living high on monies gleaned from others," controls the lives of those who can never fully repay the high interest on his loans. After watching the lavish life led by the wealthy presented alongside the poor in their tenement rooms, one critic marveled at the selfishness of the villain who "fattens on the misfortunes of his fellow beings."[21]

Like the wheat king in Griffith's earlier film, the villain was destroyed by a twist of fate involving his own greed. He reveled sensuously in the money stored in his vault when one of his clients fell in a faint against the steel door, entombing him with his money. A title card sermonized that "all his evil gains avail him nothing now." Such title cards reminded audiences that they could take vicarious delight — and a sanctimonious pride — in the demise of those who abused their power.

Yet *The Usurer* allowed the wealthy to redeem themselves in a happy ending. After the loan shark's death, his sister discovered how he had treated his clients throughout the years. Horrified at the revelation, she canceled all their debts and restored the property that her brother had confiscated to the victims of his high-interest loans. In typically Victorian style, Griffith presented the "pure" soul of womanhood as the salvation of greedy humanity.

While many Biograph motion pictures clouded social issues with fate that intervened to transform the men Ross described as criminaloids, the Edison Studios produced films that called for overt reform, but only within the cautious ideologies of the organizations with which the company collaborated. Convinced that film must play a role in improving society, the Edison Company executives received funds from the Russell Sage Foundation to make *The Usurer's Grip* in 1912. The foundation had already sponsored a survey of movie theaters in New York in 1911, carried out by the People's Institute. The findings indicated that approximately three-quarters of movie audiences were of the working class.[22] It was with that audience in mind that the Russell Sage Foundation made *The Usurer's Grip* to warn of unscrupulous money lenders like the hero of the earlier Biograph film. The film was advertising for benevolent capitalism, in the form of stock melodrama.

The Russell Sage Foundation's film told those working-class audiences whom it had identified a year earlier that capitalistic philanthropies had the interests of the nation's poor at heart. It was a call for what the historian Gabriel Kolko interprets as the preservation during the Progressive period of "the basic social and economic relations essential to a capitalist society."[23] While working-class members like the film's struggling hero and heroine might be rescued from poverty, the existing power structure might also be rescued from the attacks on it by muckrakers and Socialists alike. Critics praised *The Usurer's Grip* for its foresight in blending realistic social messages within the context of entertainment. Louis Reeves Harrison wrote an emotional tract on *The Usurer's Grip* that indicated how effectively it had merged propaganda with entertainment. Moved by the victims of such "white-collar" criminals, Harrison condemned "the majesty of the law that values inanimate property above the human being."[24] In the tumultuous context of the Progressive period, he assured society that America's institutions could remedy themselves from the inside.

The Edison Company's collaborative films responded to the challenge given the dominant social and political order in films like *Why?* or *The Kleptomaniac* with conservative pleas for careful reform. The problems lay not in the system itself, they suggested, but simply in aberrant human behavior such as that of a usurer gone greedily berserk. The solution lay, then, in organized reform to deny such individuals power. A film like *The Usurer's Grip* proved that the new entertainment form of the cinema could be "uplifting" for the masses without threatening the institutions of the nation. "Moral uplift" became the catchphrase for reformers attempting to validate the role of the cinema. They found it in such Edison films as *The Crime of Carelessness* or *The Usurer's Grip*.

The Edison Company's first collaborative films were with the government—in 1910, the company began making motion pictures to promote governmentally sponsored reforms such as the need for pure milk. The following year, *The Awakening of John Bond* furthered the Edison Company's reputation for films with a social message. That melodrama coupled condemnation of economic greed with a warning on the threat of tuberculosis in the nation's crowded slums, a threat that routinely decimated families.

"John Bond" is an archetypal landlord who rakes in his rent collections every month, indifferent to the tenants dying from tuberculosis on his property. Like the usurer, Bond has no other concern than the size of his bank account. His "awakening" occurs when Bond's own wife is stricken with the disease through contact with one of his tenants. In an almost religious transformation, Bond becomes a generous and kindly landlord—implying again that the nation's problems are rooted in greedy individuals who simply need an act of fate to "awaken" them.

The conclusion of Edison's film, claimed a critic, "forced the recognition of the motion picture . . . as the greatest educational agency since the discovery of the printing machine."[25] Two years later, Edison's film was still in circulation as part of a series of films designed to educate the public about health and hygiene. Along with drier material with titles like *The Trail of the Germs, The Fly Pest,* and *Boil Your Water, The Awakening of John Bond* drove home a message to audiences not only about disease but about the nation's scandalously neglectful landlords.

The film package drew more than 100,000 people during the duration of the showings, which extended across the towns of the industrial Northeast, indicating that Edison's attempt to secure the educational status of film was successful.[26] It is difficult, of course, to determine what motivated audiences to see the films; quite possibly, the film series toured small communities in which citizens thirsted for any sort of entertainment. What is clear, however, is that the Edison Company's lesson in *The Awakening of John Bond* about the exploitation of tenants by absentee slumlords was not limited to casual moviegoers. An even wider audience had been found.

Such films as Edison's, of course, provided easy resolutions to difficult problems. While the company demonstrated the reformation of the upper classes, the muckraking journalist Lincoln Steffens actively tried to persuade the economic leaders of the nation to develop policies that would create more equality for the working class. The short, slightly built Steffens, always on a mission, found the process far more difficult than Edison's heroes indicated on screen. "It is like reforming drunkards," Steffens complained to a friend in the spring of 1909. "These men are drunk with power and greed and selfishness, so habitually so that, as I say, some of them are hopeless."[27] His despair made it clear that the John Bonds of the world were an exception—they were fictional or cinematic artifices that made the solution to the problems Steffens faced a seemingly simple one.

The issues that Steffens raised in his many articles on corrupt business practices, urban slums, and the growing concentration of wealth in the hands of a few were a critical part of the milieu in which films like *The Awakening of John Bond* preached their messages on reform. They attempted to restore order and a sense of control in a society ringing with indictments from all sides. While Steffens, who later became a Socialist, roundly condemned the "drunkards" in power, other film studios emulated the Edison Company's attempts at soothing the discontent that Steffens fanned.

From Chicago's Essanay Company came another tale of upper-class redemption in 1912—*The Virtue of Rags*—which again featured a cruel landlord who eventually developed a conscience. Like the victims of the money lender in *The Usurer,* and the tenants of the landlord in *The Awakening of John Bond,* the working class in *The Virtue of Rags* became the recipients of a newfound benevolence from those with power over their lives.[28] Greed, the films repeatedly pointed out, may bring wealth but not happiness or serenity, and industrial capitalism failed only when individuals forgot the essential humanity of those whose lives they controlled.

Once reminded of their responsibilities, the elites in such films could magically transform the dreary lives of their tenants or workers into "happily ever after" scenarios of the future. Thus faith in both the system and the individual's mastery of adversity absorbed protest. Yet the powerlessness of the melodramatic victims remained unchallenged.

Such morality tales were more than means of providing answers to difficult social problems. They were, of course, also a means of enhancing the respectability of the movies themselves. The influential trade journal *The Moving Picture World* even hired an in-house pastor to remind exhibitors of the lessons available in such tales. The Reverend E. Boudinot Stockton, film critic, screenwriter, and pastor, found *The Virtue of Rags* "excellent" material for sermons, whether in movie houses or churches. In a regular column headlined "Pictures in the Pulpit," the minister recommended that clergymen might use the film for lessons on "the duties of the rich and poor, and on the dangers of wealth."[29] Stockton's column was part of the larger attempt to validate the motion pictures as educational, and even religious, resources.

That task was made easier by the growing array of material that celebrated personal transformations of the nation's elite. Reliance Films' *Makers and Spenders* was an exemplary example of the conflict between "wealth versus conscience" that raised fundamental issues of class conflict and reduced them to individual crises. Written by Forrest Halsey, the film contrasted a "spending" idle class with the "making" class of working people. Its villain could have been the archetype of what Thorstein Veblen scornfully derided as "the leisure class" who depended on status symbols for self-worth.[30] Surrounding himself in luxury — a shiny automobile, several maids, an elaborate home — the "spender" of the film's title had, in reality, lost his fortune. To save himself from bankruptcy, he attempted to marry off his daughter to a young millionaire who owned a local factory. "If you land Crane and his money," he wheedled his daughter Edith, "I'll be saved."

Halsey's film did not stop at criticism of the false values of the "spenders." *Makers and Spenders* took an unexpected turn from "criminaloids" like its villain to striking workers. After a heart attack claimed her father, Edith decided not to marry Crane but rather to work at his factory. "My life has been a sham," she decided. "Now I'll work for a living." What followed was an intriguing and sympathetic story of the plight of working women, as Edith soon learned that being a "maker" was not the easy task she had romanticized. When a supervisor sexually harassed one of her fellow workers, Edith led the outraged women on a strike. Police wielding nightsticks met them outside the factory, but Crane dashed in at the last minute to save Edith from being arrested. He fired the offensive supervisor, dismissed the police, rehired the women at higher wages, and, after the pattern of melodrama, married Edith.

Despite the conventional resolution of *Makers and Spenders*, however, the film contained elements of a critique of the American class structure. The "spending" class was seen as parasitical, dependent on the honest labor of the "makers," who were, in turn, exploited both sexually and economically at the workplace. The problems, then, became not the product of a single corrupt individual like John Bond but rather those of a larger system that devalued both labor and women. The presence of the police was an ominous force, not a protective one—they were enforcers not of law but of inequality and economic interests. They too were bound up in serving the interests of those in power. Though the resolution of the film's crises depended on Crane, the millionaire factory owner, the film revealed women workers expressing their discontent, actively protesting their working conditions. They were not passive victims, even when confronted with the police.

Had Thorstein Veblen ever had the opportunity to chat with Forrest Halsey, the author of *Makers and Spenders*, the two men might have discovered that their works shared at least a few similarities of thought. Veblen, an eccentric academic who cared little for conformity, and Halsey, a screenwriter who used political ideals to please the public in his films, both indicated a common scorn for what Veblen called "conspicuous consumption." *Makers and Spenders* preached about the selfishness of the idle rich, and contrasted that image with the hardworking, generous factory owner. Veblen, ever the maverick, delivered his own message—often in a barely audible whisper—from the lecterns of colleges across the country. His students may well have left his lecture halls or seminar rooms to see a film like *Makers and Spenders*. It was entertainment that embedded many of their professor's controversial ideas in the mystifications of drama, where class conflict might literally be resolved in the embrace of lovers.

Makers and Spenders, then, was a far more complex ideological statement than the collaborative films made by the Edison Company, in which protest becomes a needless, futile effort. Perhaps nowhere was that message clearer than in *The Crime of Carelessness,* the Edison melodrama made in collaboration with the National Association of Manufacturers (NAM) in 1912. The film responded to tragedies such as that at the Triangle Shirtwaist Factory, where a fire killed more than 150 women and girls in 1908. NAM funded Edison to produce a melodrama that sought vindication of the corporate system. The resulting film urged responsibility on the part of both factory workers and owners. Both the Edison film and *Makers and Spenders,* however, suggested that a younger generation of corporate owners could spawn a new kind of capitalism that served workers' needs, thus heralding an end to the "criminaloids" exposed in both the press and the cinema.

Yet the headlines pointed to an even more overt manipulating of power—that of elected officials. If the films about economic inequality contained complex messages about the nature of class conflict in America, melodramas about political corruption offered ways in which government might purge itself of elected "criminaloids." In 1911, one New York film critic reminded filmmakers that the subject was ripe for the cinema. "The alleged crimes of Tammany as regards to civic administration of this city, could all be arranged by a competent producer, photographer,.and shown on the screen."[31] It was a challenge taken up by filmmakers, and the tales of economic reform were soon paralleled in the cinema by films appealing for political reform. Edward Ross had suggested to his readers in 1909 that change must reach further than the economic sphere, since the political machinery of the nation's cities were fraught with corruption. Filmmakers, it seemed, responded to the challenges of both cinema critics and scholarly observers such as Ross.

Melodramas with the titles *The Power of the Press* (1909), *One Is Business, the Other Crime* (1908) *A Dainty Politician* (1910), *The Reform Candidate* (1911), *Exposed by the Dictograph* (1912), *The Judge's Vindication* (1913), *Her Big Story* (1913), *The Grafters* (1913), *On the Minute* (1914), *The Man of the Hour* (1914), *How Callahan Cleaned Up Little Hell* (1915), *The Politicians* (1915), and *Cy Whittacker's Ward* (1917)[32] put their "criminaloids" directly on the screen in the form of political or corporate culprits. The melodramas blamed "machine politics" for the existence of the problems of alcoholism, disease-ridden tenements, white slavery, and hazardous working conditions—all the subjects of social protest. This time, it was the people themselves who brought down such political bosses as those of Tammany Hall or the notoriously corrupt Chicago machine, who stymied democratic processes with stuffed ballot boxes and bribery. Like the melodramas about class conflict, such films were a way of proving the endurance of American institutions while allowing a channel for protest.

The Vitagraph Company's *The Power of the Press,* adapted from a play first produced in 1891, pitted the corrupt mayor of "Griggsville"—a small town set in the American West—against the new editor of the town's newspaper. Looking like bandits from the Wild West in their broad-brimmed hats and mustaches, the mayor's council tried to bribe the editor. His refusal to be corrupted infuriated them so much that they abducted him. Tipped off by the mayor's pretty niece, the sheriff rescued the editor, and *The Power of the Press*—a cross between a western and a melodrama—ended with the embrace of the heroic journalist and the young woman. Vitagraph's film won applause from the New York *Dramatic Mirror,* whose critic praised its "sense of reality"[33] and the *Moving Picture World* reviewer, who observed the use of political material in the cinema. Such cinematic portrayals of "incidents of daily life," he noted, indicated that "there is an inexhaustible supply of subjects for the adept producer."[34]

A consistent subtheme of the political graft films placed women in the role of heroines who unraveled detective stories that exposed the politician as the villain. *The Reform Candidate,* for instance, featured a feisty female reporter whom one critic praised as the sort "who has to fight her way instead of having it prepared for her; the kind of up-to-date heroine that American audiences admire more than the clinging vine variety."[35] In *Her Big Story,* a woman journalist again uncovered the real power behind the mayor. He was, ironically, also the owner of the newspaper for which she worked. The wife of a corrupt businessman in *One is Business, the Other Crime* insisted that her husband cease his involvement in political bribery. The female star of Selig's *The Scales of Justice* became the source of tension between an honest politician and the political "boss" for the ward when both fell in love with her. The heroine chose the honest man, at which point the corrupt boss fired him. But together the newly married couple exposed his trickery and brought him to trial. The "scales of justice" weighed the wrongs of the American political machinery, and in the fashion that movie audiences like to believe, individuals corrected injustice.

The social problem films dealing with corruption in high places presented drastically different images of women. They ranged from the Victorian "clinging vine" to the independent, assertive characters who dethroned powerful figures. The cinematic portrayals of women reflected a society slowly relinquishing a nineteenth-century code of female behavior and roles—and they also encouraged that relinquishment. As women took on larger activities outside the home, in workplaces or in political organizations, they found fictional counterparts on movie screens to provide role models. It was, as a reviewer stated, a "new age" in politics, and women were on hand to actively usher it in,[36] particularly in such movements as the temperance and suffrage causes.

When *The Judge's Vindication* or *A Dainty Politician* explored problems of corruption in political circles, and settled them with romantic or individualized solutions, critics voiced their approval of what they saw as realistic portrayals of the situation. In 1910, immediately following the release of *A Dainty Politician,* a critic guessed that "someone connected with the studio [Thanhouser] had learned something of ward politics, and the methods of controlling a convention are very clearly and bluntly stated."[37] Three years later, when Reliance Films released *The Judge's Vindication,* the political situation remained unchanged, and yet another reviewer suggested that the film would be a success precisely because it dealt with the issues that newspapers publicized. The film's interest, he wrote, "comes from the fact that there is so much in it that is natural and in accord with what we all have read in newspaper accounts of political life."[38] This was one source of the films' popularity: in the transformation of "news" into fantasy lay a mechanism for creating a sense of order. Despite the troubles presented in the nation's headlines, then, the America of the cinema was essentially orderly and its conflicts controllable.

The expectation, of course, that motion pictures should be in "accordance" with the newspapers was a naive critical assumption. Yet the effectiveness of political melodramas depended on how well they presented themselves as accurate indicators of the problem. The minister and film reviewer E. Boudinot Stockton criticized the "farcical element" he found in films about political graft that undermined their call for reform. What was needed, he believed, were more films like World Films' *The Man of the Hour,* produced in 1913. Adapted from a play by George Broadhurst, the film starred a corrupt political boss and his cohort. They were brought down by an honest politician whose own father was ruined by the villain. The settings, Stockton noted, heightened the believability of the film, which "forces home to the spectator in a most telling way the reality of what is being enacted."[39]

Stockton could not have imagined how much more real the enactment of political films would become two years later. In 1915 William Sulzer made *The Governor's Boss* to dramatize his own impeachment as governor of New York. Yet the film bridged the gulf between the actual historical incidents it portrayed and the conventions of the melodrama by resolving the conflict romantically. Bowing to the convention of the "happy ending," it restored democracy to the hands of the people. Its fantastic conclusion tended to mystify the problems it raised, rendering the film a less powerful weapon against Tammany. As Bertolt Brecht would later insist, the relationship of art to society must be that of "a hammer, not a mirror"—but Sulzer's use of the new art of the motion picture attempted both roles.[40] While *The Governor's Boss* was a weapon against political corruption, it was also a reflection of the melodramatic sentimentality of its era.

Whether the "criminaloids" gained their illegal power economically or politically, the films they inspired showed their demise or their redemption. They assured the public that America would not tolerate their control over the lives of average men and women. The democratic process would prevail over the threats from inside the system. Frederic Howe's vision of a radical cinema catering to the interests of organized discontents or flaming radicals never came to pass in America, although occasional films like *Makers and Spenders* and *The Kleptomaniac* exposed the inequities in the class structure. A film like *Why?,* then, remained an anomaly in its celebration of the masses and revolutionary rather than individual, subtle change. Though Socialists debated the viability of capitalism during the Progressive period, the years in which the film industry developed belonged more to those appealing for cautious reform that allowed continuity instead of disruption.

The redemptive or reformative portrait of those "criminals of greed," whom Edward Ross analyzed and denounced, was only one image of inequality in the cinema. Other melodramas focused on the victims of the criminaloid—those who lived in the tenements or those unjustly confined in prisons. These films graphically showed, as the journalist Jacob Riis titled his famous book just at the close of the nineteenth century, "how the other half lives."

CHAPTER 2

A Cinema
of the Submerged

With a despairing cry, he gathered his family into his arms.
Let the warders come now, if they wanted to. What was a prison
cell in the face of this?
—*Escaped from Sing-Sing*, 1905

The short, bespectacled journalist Jacob Riis, whose photographs and exposés of urban poverty had shaken the country's conscience, stood at the rear of a movie house in New York City in the spring of 1907. He was not there to condemn the nickelodeons, as had many of his fellow reformers, such as Jane Addams. Nor had he come to pass an evening idly watching the movies. His time was much too precious for that. Instead, Jacob Riis himself was the star attraction that night—or at least his slide show was. He was making use of the public forum provided for causes such as his by the city's new movie houses.

Billed as "The Battle of the Slums," after Riis's second book, the stereopticon slides illustrated what the journalist called "the evil offspring of public neglect and private greed."[1] The photographs that Riis had taken of the city's slum dwellers flashed across the screen as he spoke to a hushed audience. The crowd he drew was not an ordinary nickelodeon crowd: his audience had come to catch a glimpse of the city's poverty-stricken "other half," and the horrors that unfolded on the screen before them startled them more than any film melodrama they may have casually seen as middle-class moviegoers. Staggered by the revelation of such poverty, one film reviewer informed his readers that the talk "on the 'submerged' 10th of New York was one of such a nature as almost beggared belief."[2]

Though Riis's entry into the world of the New York cinema may have been unusual on that spring night in 1907, the exposure of his subject matter in movie houses was not. Riis was part of the milieu of muckraking journalism that at times found expression — sometimes directly — in the fledgling cinema. His photojournalistic investigations of those he called "the submerged," "the other half," or "the children of the tenements" helped to influence a budding subgenre of motion picture melodramas.

His terms even became titles of melodramas: *The Submerged,* released by Essanay Films in 1912, featured a wealthy young man who rejected his upper-class sweetheart when she sneered at the people standing in breadlines. Instead, he married a destitute young woman and carried her off like some twentieth-century Cinderella into the elite circles of old Eastern wealth. But it was not that happy ending that won critical attention. Instead, as one reviewer observed, it was the fact that the camera brought audiences "in touch with people 'in the breadline' and with pampered society folks who have never known the pinch of want."[3] Despite the union between the rich and poor in the closure, it was the film's contrast of the classes in America that impressed the critic James S. McQuade; he saw its message as one that showed how "poverty begats sympathy and wealth has the tendency to breed selfishness and apathy."[4]

A 1904 collection of Jacob Riis's stories, *Children of the Tenements,* inspired a film with that title released in 1913 by the Kalem Company. The film version attempted precise journalistic coverage, reporting that thousands of New York children — 26,000, to be exact — living in the dense tenement districts had only the streets as their playgrounds.[5] *The Other Half,* released in 1912 by Thanhouser Films in collaboration with the New York Association for Improving the Conditions of the Poor, again dramatized issues originally publicized by Riis, and was designed to display the need for organized charity.[6]

Riis was not the only muckraking journalist to see his ideas animated with motion pictures. When Upton Sinclair collaborated with All-Star Pictures in 1913 to bring his novel *The Jungle* to the movie screen, it was with the hope of raising funds for his broadly based work for social justice in America. In its five reels, Sinclair played the part of a Socialist crusader (based loosely on Eugene Debs) who won over the film's hero to socialism.[7] The hero saw the tragic consequences of the meat-packing industry both on workers and on consumers. At one dramatic point in the film, a worker fell into a vat of boiling lard, which was then poured into cans for consumption. Sinclair's cinematic portrayal of the illness and suffering caused by the greed of the meat-packing industry won, however, neither the financial nor critical success he anticipated. *Variety*'s critic sneered at the film and at those whom he called "Sinclair's I.W.W.'s." Obviously biased against Sinclair's political sympathies, he exposed vicious anti-Wobbly sentiment in the film review, writing that perhaps one reason the workers didn't attend the film was because they all had night jobs; "although why the I.W.W.'s should prefer night work if ever laboring, one couldn't imagine, unless it is that their whiskers don't seem so horrid in the dark."[8]

According to at least one worker who took the time to write Sinclair, however, *The Jungle* was a powerful instigator not only for reform of the meat-packing industry. This member of *The Jungle*'s audience, an Illinois tailor, gave a lively description of the film's effect. In a letter that must have heartened Sinclair, the tailor wrote that "about 350 people attended [the screening] and if the picture man had it better advertised good many more would seen it. . . . Next time we will have twise as many to see it . . . caused a sausage and lard strike for weeks after. Good many trowed al their lard and sausage away. . . . It made Socialists of many, specely of the young people."[9] Hoping for similar reactions to his film, Sinclair took the print of *The Jungle* and distributed it to individual Socialist groups until the print finally wore out.

Both *The Jungle* and the films using Riis's work indicated how messages for social change could be woven into entertainment—and how deeply intertwined, even inseparable, ideology and entertainment became. Like the motion pictures exposing "criminaloids," the cinema of the submerged pointed to ruptures in the economic and social order. One of the functions of the motion pictures was that the extraordinary—that which "beggared belief"—began to seem ordinary, of the realm of everyday life. Though the melodramas were clear-cut calls for reform, they also indicated that poverty's victims were ordinary people who would passively endure their lot in life. Sinclair's film was unusual in its call for a Socialist alternative. Most of the films based on Riis's work suggested that change would be slow. The films were clear-cut examples of how motion pictures could serve as advocates of change that would be acceptable to the middle classes.

Such films reassured their audiences that, although the dichotomy between rich and poor in America might be very real, it was not a yawning gulf filled hopelessly with eternal class conflict. In contrast to the stark reality Jacob Riis brought directly into the theater with his "magic lantern" shows, melodramas translated the journalist's photographs into pathos and palatable entertainment.

When the early filmmakers attempted to make their craft as realistic as possible, they dramatized heroes and heroines stepping from the slums of the nation's cities, from small struggling farms, from sweatshops, and even from prisons like the notorious Sing-Sing to reveal the plight of hapless victims of injustice and inequality. But while Riis called for immediate attention to such problems, the films offered their own solutions, which tended to defuse the power of their statements. The protagonists often escaped their troubles through a lucky brush with the upper classes in resolutions reminiscent of the sort popularized by Horatio Alger's tales. Still other melodramas told of grimmer fates awaiting their characters. Endurance, not change, and passivity, not activity, were the keys to survival. While Riis made overtly political uses of the motion picture theater, filmmakers romanticized his concerns in melodramas that capitalized on the climate of reform.

The film titles themselves promised stories of compassion: *A Child of the Ghetto* (1910), *A Convict's Sacrifice* (1908), *Poverty and Probity* (1908), *The Helping Hand* (1908), *A Convict's Heart* (1911), and *Mother's Crime* (1908) constructed worlds in which the poor either triumphed or proudly endured their fates. Here were plots in which destitute mothers stole to feed their children, escaped convicts allowed poor children to turn them in so the children could pay their parents' mortgage with the reward money, and young women in breadlines converted greedy millionaires into generous philanthropists.

Perhaps more important than their romantic resolutions, however, was the fact that these films continued to bring the problems of the day before the public. Despite their easy solutions, the films that championed the underclasses ensured that inequality and the need for social reforms were not forgotten. In 1907, the wealthy Socialist and newspaper heir Joseph Medill Patterson observed the way movie theaters flourished in the city ghettoes. He optimistically predicted that motion pictures were "an effective protagonist of democracy," most suited to the slums where they were "fittest" and could thrive.[10] There was a contradiction in Patterson's idea. He romanticized the early "democratizing" role of the motion pictures while, in the language of social Darwinism, he suggested that their survival depended on the existence of the slum. Yet he also made a significant observation, touching on the films' importance for those to whom the "American Dream" still remained an elusive ideal. The films told many of their working-class viewers that life, indeed, might be miserable and the world cold, but inside movie theaters, empathy and understanding could be found for the price of admission. Some films were made specifically for communities within the ghettoes: the proletarian Jews, for instance, were the heroes of A Man's a Man (1912) and Children of the Ghetto (1915).[11]

The films of those whom Riis termed "the submerged" touched a fundamental human need: they celebrated the dignity and self-worth of their characters as they faced adversity. These apparently simple stories laid bare the failures of industrial society and dismissed the idea that poverty was a personal flaw—the traditional American values surrounding the Protestant work ethic that blamed the lower-class individual for his or her place in society. Instead, the outside forces that kept the "submerged" in place were explored in a series of films that raised questions about justice in America.

Tales of ex-convicts, for instance, often lifted the prisoners to the status of hard-working heroes who had lost their jobs and been railroaded into jail. Typically, however, the plots tempered their social criticism by only alluding to the need for reform of the legal and penal systems. Instead, they implied that it was their heroes' fate to endure rather than resist the wrongs they suffered.

Geared to audiences in city ghettoes, the films dealt sympathetically with the criminal as ex-convict. Edwin S. Porter directed one of the first melodramas in that chain of films. In 1904, his film The Ex-Convict elevated its protagonist into a martyred and ultimately heroic figure. Though technically crude (each of eight "episodes" consisted of a single scene filmed by a stationary camera) for the time period, the attempt to tell a fairly complicated narrative story was ambitious. The first several scenes revealed the hero meeting one failure after another, moving from prison release to reunion with his family to, finally, rejection by potential employers. The stigma of his conviction clung to him as if he still wore prison stripes. The audience was never told of his crime; the point was the hero's present condition and the overwhelming prejudice against him. Even when the hero finally found employment, a policeman whispered of his background to his boss, and he was immediately fired. Society in such films became a web of conspiracy against those struggling for reasonable wages and for respect. Crime became an activity into which the poor were forced by an economic system that closed them out. While Porter's film ended happily, it was through an act of fate: the hero found a wealthy benefactor when he rescued the man's daughter from an oncoming automobile. Though this kind of the closure would shift in later films, the problems faced by the ex-convict remained in place, to be worked out cinematically many times.

Immediately following Porter's film with the Edison Company, Vitagraph Films released *Escaped from Sing-Sing* in early 1905. Its hero escaped from the notorious prison of the film's title to rejoin his wife and children in the country. During the escape scenes, a title card informed the audience that "cruel enemies who had told lies" had caused the hero's prison sentence.[12] Unlike Porter's hero, however, there was no justice in store for the Sing-Sing escapee: in a shoot-out at his home, police killed one of his young daughters and forced his surrender. "What was a prison cell," he asked himself, "in the face of this?" His family literally and figuratively destroyed, the escapee from Sing-Sing returned to that infamous prison where jail cells held others, according to the film, as unfairly accused as he.

Vitagraph continued its cinematic challenges to an ineffectual, discriminatory legal system with *Mother's Crime* in 1908, in which a judge sentenced a woman to prison for stealing food for her starving daughter, and *Courage of Sorts* in 1911, featuring a physician wrongfully convicted of a crime.[13] Even professional men and desperate mothers could fall victim to the travesty that, according to these films, the American system of justice had become. Other companies joined Vitagraph's melodramatic bandwagon with motion pictures that critiqued the legal system by showing the scorn given its individual victims. American film companies such as Edison, Reliance, Biograph, Selig, and Essanay all found the ex-convict a sympathetic and colorful hero. With *The Convict's Bridge* (1906), *The Prisoner's Escape* (1907), *Ex-Con #900* (1910), *A Convict's Heart* (1911), *The Ones Who Suffer* (1911), *The Redeemed Criminal* (1911), *His Chance to Make Good* (1912), *Bread upon the Water* (1912), *The Ex-Con* (1912), *Self-Convicted* (1913), *The Fight for Freedom* (1908), *A Little Child* (1909), or *In Convict Garb* (1913), films captured the pathos of the lonely prisoner's attempt to find a new place in a hostile world.[14] Like Edwin S. Porter's *The Kleptomaniac,* these films criticized the social order. According to their plots, poor wages or unemployment drove their heroes and heroines to illegal acts in order to survive. The legal system in turn punished them for those efforts, and then public prejudice refused them reentry into society.

In 1909, Biograph released a melodrama that suggested the flaws lay in the legal system itself, as well as in societal attitudes. *Was Justice Served?* asked whether the jury system could work successfully when discrimination ran high against those with prison records. In its opening scenes, a newly released prisoner changed into civilian clothes with hopes of beginning his life anew with his wife. Yet, because a thief planted a stolen wallet on him while he rested from his job search, the hero found himself once again in the custody of the police. Like their cinematic counterparts in *A Legal Hold-Up* and *How They Rob Men in Chicago,* the police officers themselves were criminals in uniforms. They ransacked the hero's home and threw his wife to the floor when she protested their illegal search for evidence. The trial was equally a sham, but fortunately for the hero, an ironic twist intervened: the actual thief sat nervously on the jury. Haunted by a guilty conscience, he cast the only vote for acquittal. Had it not been for an act of fate, the legal system would have sent an innocent man to jail. As it was, the real criminal went free and the police went unreprimanded, thus inviting the question raised in the film's title.

So inflammatory was the film's challenge to the legal system that one critic rose to the defense of American justice. Justice would *indeed* have been served, insisted W. Stephen Bush, even had the innocent hero been convicted.[15] The evidence, after all, pointed to his guilt. The sequence of melodramas that championed the ex-convict presented an unsettling view of American life from the bottom. The shadows they cast on the country's most revered institutions added ammunition to the arguments of those who would censor the cinema.

The films were sufficiently critical of the country's most sacrosanct institutions to upset legislators. In 1913, several politicians in South Dakota unsuccessfully introduced a bill that would have made it illegal for any motion picture to show the act of "resisting an officer."[16] The proposal suggested that films wielded the power to influence not only opinion but behavior. Such explicit censorship, however, was probably not necessary. By 1913, filmmakers had moved increasingly toward suggesting more middle-class solutions to social problems. The issues like those explored in the ex-convict series became channeled into cinematic calls for social reform, which slowly began to replace the visceral appeals to mass audiences. For instance, Kaybee Films' 1914 gangster film, *The Gangsters and the Girl,* featured the daughter of a Sing-Sing convict who stole to raise money for his legal fees. By the end of the film, however, she was thoroughly absorbed into the middle class, graduating from business college and marrying a policeman. While earlier films protested what they saw as a bigoted society, *The Gangsters and the Girl* asserted America's ability to reward the virtuous.

In the summer of 1913, Reliance Films released one of the most powerful dramas for prison reform, *The Fight for Right.* The film featured a middle-class heroine rather than the working-class heroes of earlier films. Like similar motion pictures dealing with political graft, *The Fight for Right* starred a woman. Its heroine led the movement against the politicians whose interests were served by convict labor. Scripted by James Oppenheim, a Progressive reformer who first studied prison conditions before embarking on the screenplay for his film, the film suggested that corrupt politicians were responsible for the convict labor system. It also suggested that the women's reform movement could be a central force in exposing those wrongs. While others of the prison subgenre relegated their heroes to passive martyrdom, *The Fight for Right* forged beyond simple commentary on social conditions. It made a statement about what reforms were necessary to bring about real change.

Coming as it did at a time when the film industry increasingly collaborated with reform groups to make self-consciously socially "respectable" films, *The Fight for Right* won the endorsement of the National Committee on Prison Labor. It also won critical praise, including a two-page spread, complete with stills, from the *Moving Picture World.* Its critic hailed the film's "assistance in [the] fight for better conditions in state prisons."[17] Ultimately, the film popularized the idea of prison reform in a commercial fashion that capitalized on melodramatic conventions. James Oppenheim himself later turned the ideas of Carl Jung into a parlor game that he marketed as "Know Your Type."[18] In a sense, his film performed the same service in 1913. It delivered an important idea to the public as entertainment for the middle classes. It took an already popular film subject — that of the ex-convict's plight—and put a middle-class heroine in the plot, transforming working-class material into an appealing subject for newer film audiences. The same was true of *The Governor's Double,* released by Patheplay in 1913. In that film, the New York governor had himself sentenced to jail "to investigate prison conditions" and changed roles with a convict he had just pardoned.[19]

The new elevation of the criminal to the stature of hero roused controversy among those, like the members of the South Dakota legislature, who feared its effect on young audiences. But the films also demonstrated a need for prison reform and public understanding of the position of those with a prison record. Those needs were documented by the works of Progressives such as James Hopper, a novelist and journalist of the era. In 1909, Hopper created a sensation with the publication of his novel *9009* (titled for the number worn by its hero in prison). Thomas Osborne became another real-life hero crusading for better prisons; his books *Within Prison Walls* and *Society and Prisons,* published in 1914 and 1916, probed inside penitentiary walls and found nearly incredible scenes.

So pervasive was that socially concerned climate during the early years of the film industry that D. W. Griffith remembered its influence with a caustic barb in his memoirs. Nearly four decades later, the aging director recalled that "a great wave of reform was sweeping the countryside at the time. . . . You could tell how sincere the papers were by the way they were working from the ground up—in spreading the pictures of these underpinnings all over the front pages. There were campaigns against everything." He added sarcastically, "So I decided to help reform the moving picture business."[20]

Though Griffith refused to join forces with those whom one of his films called *The Reformers: or, The Lost Art of Minding One's Own Business,* in 1913 he consistently directed melodramas that called attention to the plight of the working classes as the nation industrialized. Such films demonstrated, as he later put it, "the triumph" of "ordinary virtues" that involved "no socialism."[21] His films contained implicit criticisms of the manner in which American industrialization forgot the ordinary American virtues he extolled. In 1908, he followed a pattern already begun with Edwin S. Porter's *The Kleptomaniac;* Griffith helped to usher in a series of tragic melodramas that elevated the submerged into sympathetic heroes or heroines. Other film companies rode the popular tide until it began to ebb with the decline of the

Progressive era and with economic changes in the film industry itself. The initially shocking vision of poverty and inequality lost its power as it became clichéd through the years. But in the context of reform prior to World War I, the stories of the submerged were a virtual subgenre of melodrama for which Griffith was largely responsible. In 1908, Biograph used Jacob Riis's famous term for the proletariat — the "other half" — in its promotion of Griffith's *The Song of the Shirt*, released within only a few months of the journalist's traveling slide show. The melodrama added a new, cynical twist to Riis's words with a bulletin announcing that "one half the world doesn't know how the other gets along, nor," it added ominously, "does it care."[22] The film is significant not only because it indicates influence by Riis's ideas, but because its plot incorporated themes developed many times in the "cinema of the submerged" in the years following its release.

Less an overt call for reform than the Kalem film, *Children of the Tenements, The Song of the Shirt* revealed the struggle of the poor merely to survive despite the exploitation of their condition by greedy industrialists. Featuring Florence Lawrence, who would soon become the first celebrated star of the moving picture industry, the film proceeded to tell a sordid tale of labor conditions and tenement misery.

Lawrence, whose face projected both strength and fragility, played an orphaned seamstress in *The Song of the Shirt*. The opening scene quickly established which half of the world would receive sympathy in the film, as Lawrence bent over her sick sister in their tenement room. A sewing machine loomed in the background — an icon indicating the only means of economic survival for the two sisters. A cut to the "Acme Waist Company" revealed the heroine, described by the bulletin as a "Weak, wan, emaciated slip of famininity [sic]"[23] pleading for work from indifferent factory owners who waved her out the door.

Using the parallel editing techniques that he later developed in more sophisticated form in *A Corner in Wheat* and, in 1915, in *The Birth of a Nation*, Griffith illuminated the discrepancy between America's "two halves." The audience immediately saw a cut from the factory owners back to the invalid sister, heaving in the death throes from tuberculosis. The camera immediately cut back to the factory. The men finally agreed to give the heroine a parcel of sewing to do, shaking a warning finger at her for promptness and perfection.

Meanwhile, the company president reveled in pleasure with two showgirls. The contrast between the three merrymakers, lifting their champagne glasses, and the heroine, treading away at her sewing machine, needed no words to explain that, in Griffith's eyes, the wealthy did not care about the plight of the poor. Even a title card would have been superfluous.

More graphic was Griffith's final scene: the manager arrived at the tenement and refused to pay the heroine because of a slightly imperfect seam. He left Lawrence sobbing on the body of her sister, dead from the disease of the tenements. The grim tale could have stepped directly from Riis's own collection of true but sentimentally told stories in *Children of the Tenements* — yet Griffith's editorial commentary silently appealed to the visceral, with its abrupt visual movement between what Biograph called the "two halves" of society.

Yet it was hardly a drive for "reform" that first led Griffith into filmmaking. Desperate for money at age thirty-one, the tall, dignified Griffith stooped to find work in the "disreputable" film industry. In the spring of 1908, he and his wife, a dark-haired actress named Linda Arvidson, walked with trepidation into the American Mutoscope and Biograph Film Studio in New York City. Moving pictures, thought Arvidson, were "cheap and tawdry;"[24] after all, "decent" people did not frequent nickelodeons. Yet she and her husband knew that struggling actors like themselves often found financial reward working in those "galloping tintypes," as Griffith scornfully called films.[25] Times were rough for the couple, and Griffith had decided that perhaps acting in and writing for the movies might subsidize their theater careers. For the time, at least, they would lower themselves into the lucrative world of New York's "canned dramas."

It was, of course, a fortunate move for both D. W. Griffith and the film industry. The films Griffith made pioneered new aesthetic dimensions in the cinema. But his melodramas at Biograph also created new standards for subject matter as well as technique. The arch conservative Griffith helped pioneer the motion pictures dealing with social problems, with his melodramatic versions of how industrial capitalism affected the individual. Couched as they were in the framework of Victorianism, Griffith's films set a pattern for the popularity of melodramas that explored the conditions of growing industrialization and class inequality.

As a young man, Griffith had experienced firsthand life in New

York's Bowery district. What he saw there revealed itself in his numerous melodramas set in inner city slums. His leading star and protégée, Lillian Gish, later recalled the sincerity of Griffith's interest in the people represented in his tenement dramas. He was, she remembered, "deeply sympathetic to the sufferings of the poor, to the injustices inflicted upon them."[26] Those sympathies were clearly expressed in the themes that Griffith promoted time and again. Despite his tongue-in-cheek barbs at the "great wave of reform," Griffith borrowed his ideas not only from the New York streets and from novelists like Stephen Crane and Frank Norris, but from the journalistic reformers such as Jacob Riis, who sought to change urban life.

Out of Biograph Studios, where Griffith worked, poured countless films dealing with, as a film bulletin for *The Two Sides* put it, the "vivid contrast of the world's prosperous and poor."[27] Griffith conveyed an antimodern sensibility that revealed a spontaneous empathy for the farmers, the factory workers, or the tenement dwellers. Whether he situated his heroes and heroines in urban slums or in the rural outposts of the South, they often became victims of an economic system contrary to that of the Old South that Griffith romanticized so vividly in *The Birth of a Nation*. *A Child of the Ghetto* (1910), *'Tis an Ill Wind* (1909), *The Message of the Violin* (1910), *The Helping Hand* (1908), *A Trap for Santa Claus* (1909) or *The Musketeers of Pig Alley* (1912), among many other melodramas, told stories of despair in the tenements or in factories without unions—until romance and financial success proved that luck could look favorably even on those trapped in exploitative situations. Impressed by their social statements, one reporter claimed that Griffith's melodramas took a step above the usual level of entertainment. Instead, the films were "a wholly new departure both in pictures and in editorials."[28] Defying conventional labels, the films, he thought, could be called "picture-editorials," filled with the conflicts in the nation's ghettoes. Griffith himself noted that, when he moved from Kentucky to New York as a young man, the city streets of the ghetto "never appeared like a melting pot to me. It seemed more like a boiling pot."[29]

That sense of conflict and contradiction emerged even in Griffith's earliest films. *A Child of the Ghetto* showed a young orphan escaping her cruel boss in a shirt factory.[30] *A Trap for Santa Claus* raised the issues of unemployment, alcoholism, poverty, and crime, only to resolve them all in its heroine's sudden inheritance. Nuances abounded in the film as the heroine forgave her husband for his desperate descent into crime. Messages about the martyred role of women, fate, the emptiness of wealth without love, and the act of crime as a sometimes necessary act of survival made *A Trap for Santa Claus* an ideologically complex film. It implicitly challenged the work ethic, the status brought by money and consumerism, and made crime a product of poverty.

Such stories, apparently, could be endlessly told to moviegoers as the plots transformed the lives of the "submerged." Audiences wanted to see realistic hardships, believed a film commentator for *Moving Picture World,* who based his observation on the reactions of nickelodeon audiences in 1908. "Films," stressed Burton Allbee, "which are somewhat pathetic in nature seem to be favorites."[31] The public, he thought, "want themselves" as the heroes and heroines of their entertainment. The clichés and archetypes of what critics called the "pathetic melodrama" became such because they originally touched a psychological nerve in the public. They represented a need to control— indeed, to travel beyond—the limits of everyday life. The scenarios confirmed the experiences of working-class audiences (who, as observers put it in 1907 and again in 1910, could afford the cheaper form of drama)[32] but also lifted those moviegoers out of daily life, allowing them visions of an America that still promised endless opportunity, of a world in which fate could intervene to ensure that justice might be won for those living in the nation's ghettoes.

Such dark—though ultimately redemptive—struggles in American life as those animated by Griffith and his counterparts at other studios finally inspired one film critic to throw up his hands in disgust. Writing in 1911, William Kitchell complained humorously about the growing concentration on bleak reality. "There is enough tragedy in life without running it into the pictures," he argued. "Most of us get enough tragedy in the morning newspapers."[33] Trying to inject levity into the subject of dire melodramas, Kitchell went on to speculate that "if a man is known by the films he manufactures, more than one motion picture capitalist was born in a morgue and has camped out ever since in some backwoods graveyard."[34] Yet Kitchell's criticism did nothing to staunch the flow of the melodramas, even though a year later another weary critic, Louis Reeves Harrison, sighed that "mother is still unable to pay the rent in a large number of recent heart-rending photosobs."[35] Such critical protests indicated that the old melodramatic formula, with its familiar plot, archetypes, and icons, needed modern inventions to remain entertaining. Yet the films continued to explore the problems of powerlessness and poverty, representing a cinema addressed to underclasses who found entertainment that validated their suffering, implicitly questioned its cause, and often alleviated it in romance.

In 1912, Griffith released a film that used the conventions criticized by Kitchell but also transcended them. In *The Musketeers of Pig Alley,* he produced a motion picture that drew on the stereotypes about the ghetto but avoided the easy closures of his earlier tenement films. The film showed its characters without escape in the trap of the ghetto, briefly enjoying its saloons and dance halls, but struggling — honest workers and gangsters alike — to gain power over their lives. Featuring Lillian Gish and Walter Miller as the leading couple, the plot revealed Miller as a poor musician in conflict with the ghetto hoodlums, led by the "Snapper Kid," the "Chief of the Musketeers." The couple struggled to regain money stolen from them by the gangster. During a shoot-out in an alley — an episode in "The Gangsters' Feudal War" — the hero fought with the "Snapper Kid" and recovered his wallet. The ending was more cynical than Griffith's usual romantic or redemptive closure: the honest couple agreed to provide an alibi for the "Snapper Kid." After the gangster pleaded for sympathy, the couple lied to a policeman about his involvement in the shoot-out. One of the final scenes revealed what a title card called "links in the system," as the policeman and the gangster exchanged glances that suggested corruption and bribery.

The ending left the viewer without the feeling of either continuity or surrender that many of Griffith's other films provided. A disquieting, ominous tone pervaded *The Musketeers of Pig Alley* that, as the film historian William K. Everson has noted, precursed the later gangster films.[36] In it, Griffith portrayed a world in which the hero circumvented the police, and the gangsters themselves appeared to be victims of the ghetto. The Biograph bulletin released along with the film advertised that the melodrama "showed the gangster evil" and "the extreme necessity for radical action on the part of the authorities," meaning that reform was urgent.[37] Without an honest police force and an effective legal system to remedy the structural flaws that allowed bribery and corruption to continue, cultures like those shown in "Pig Alley" established their own order and made their own rules.

Griffith's message was told as much by *how* he created the story as by *what* he told. Although the story opened with a foreboding title card informing audiences that they were about to venture into "New York's Other Side," it was the claustrophobic atmosphere, the sinister close-ups of the gangsters' faces, and the camera angles that created a world in which little freedom was apparent. The city streets teemed with people of all nationalities, all ethnic groups, all ages and races— a true vision of America at the turn of the century.

As Gish ventured out into the streets, the camera trailed behind her through a street narrowed by throngs of people. There, indeed, was Griffith's "boiling pot." Despite the filth and confines of the slums in *The Musketeers of Pig Alley,* the heroes and heroines were far from passive recipients of whatever fate doled out. They fought their environment, yet at the same time defended it against outside inter-lopers who appeared in the uniform of the police. The film recreated the confined world of the ghetto whose inhabitants were societal victims, first driven to preying upon themselves, then to taking their destinies into their own hands. But even in victory, the hero and heroine realized that criminals like the "Snapper Kid" were not self-made but victims of outside forces—victims weaker than them-selves. Again, Griffith left no real solution other than endurance, surrender to the forces of fate that might radically alter the lives of his characters. His films, with their fantastic solutions or their defeatist world views, suggested that real change would be a difficult process. While the films implicitly questioned the class system that fostered the conflicts on which many a melodramatic plot turned, rarely did they challenge the economic system, as Sinclair's *The Jungle* did in 1913. If the cinema raised these larger issues at all, it was to quickly dismiss them. Even films featuring Socialist heroes and heroines "reformed" them into good solid Americans who learned their lessons either in the work ethic or through romance.

The hero of *The Voice of the Violin,* a young Socialist who taught music, gave up his radical beliefs for his wealthy sweetheart. *A Million Dollars* and *Greater Wealth,* in 1912 and 1913, confused the Socialist idealism of an Upton Sinclair or an Emma Goldman with capitalist fantasies: in both films, the Socialist heroes pushed for their ideals with the ulterior motive of living off the work of others. Thus they could earn the financial rewards referred to in the titles. In happy endings, both heroes understood that life's greatest pleasure lay in the financial reward of honest hard work, not in the apparently lazy alternative of a Socialist system. That message also carried with it an antilabor sentiment. The story of *A Million Dollars* ended on a pious note: "Our employers are often far better than we give them credit for being."[38] In an age when strikers protested working conditions across the country, such a message was an undisguised attempt to plea for the cause of management.

In 1913, the authors of a screenwriting manual designed to teach novice writers the tricks of the new trade advised their readers to downplay those politically charged subjects that might offend middle-class audiences. *Writing the Photoplay* suggested that "no matter what political theme you exploit in your story, heart-interest must predominate."[39] The manual reflected a period in film history when the cinema struggled for respectability and broad audiences, and attempted to shed the stigma of working-class entertainment. Innocently, the handbook stated the crux of the social problem film's function: the problems raised might threaten the very assumptions of society—as did Riis's photographs—but the answers must lie in the taming or the privatization of those dilemmas. According to these advisers, it was better to stay away from politics altogether, even when the subject was coupled with love: "That form of journalism which is best known as muckraking," they insisted, "is also out of place in the picture."[40] In 1913, these authors feared the overtly political motion pictures made by filmmakers like Sinclair, Emmeline Pankhurst, or William Sulzer. Their challenges to an already precarious social order were, according to these advisers, outside the acceptable boundaries of cinematic entertainment.

Many of the film melodramas of this period nevertheless assumed an inherently political role in society. They defused the thrust for organizational change into a private, individual need for self-worth or romance. The films gave a certain grandeur to suffering. They held up a distorted mirror to the lives of their working class audiences and often magnified the problems there into a universal martyrdom. If martyrdom were not the answer, however, the crisis of poverty and powerlessness was easily solved by romance. Even James Oppenheim's appeal for prison reform in *The Fight for Right* concluded with a wedding between the crusading heroine and the ex-convict's brother. The most volatile of conflicts dissolved in "heart-interest"—the ultimate democratizer in America. Such endings represented the desire to believe that a safe, just world existed. Though essentially powerless, the heroes and heroines of the "submerged" dramas could trust that larger forces would intervene to justify their existence, whether as martyrs or as victors through romance.

As rosy as the romantic endings may have appeared to the audiences who kept returning to nickelodeons, those resolutions faded in the harsher light outside movie houses. Working men and women were beginning to realize in increasing numbers that more immediate change was necessary. Miners, factory workers, sweatshop seamstresses—the characters portrayed in films by beautiful heroines and handsome heroes—hoped that, in real life, labor unions might provide a direct agent for changing the problems of "capital versus labor." The films about labor unionism often revealed workers actively seeking change for themselves, in contrast to the melodramas about life in the slums, which simply allowed hardship to be endured.

Just as the "cinema of the submerged" established a portrait of the nation's powerless and needy, the films of labor unionism seized on the issues dominating the nation's headlines. But this time the movies revealed the workers fighting back—in ways that were often sensationalized. "The fight for right" was taking place in city streets, factories, in the rough mining country of the West—and in the nation's movie houses.

CHAPTER 3

Labor Unionism:
Seeds of Discontent

With a sense of having been unjustly injured,
Tony revenges himself by sowing seeds of discontent
among the other laborers.
— *One Kind of Wireless*, 1917

In the winter of 1919, the movie producer David Horsley delivered a speech to a group of labor activists and film associates in Los Angeles. He was excited about his new film company, Motive Motion Pictures, which would use fiction film to further the cause of labor unionism. The cinema, he explained to his audience, was a powerful "new force . . . which is greater than either the newspapers or magazines." With Motive Pictures, the cinema "for the first time is to be used in the interest of Organized Labor."[1] Horsley's first film would be scripted by Upton Sinclair, whose book *The Cry of Justice* had converted him to socialism.[2]

Motive Motion Pictures was an ambitious undertaking. Its vision of a labor-oriented cinema, however, never came to pass. Financial problems and the lack of cooperation of union officials prevented Horsley from making the films to promote organized labor. Yet its existence is an indication of the way in which the early cinema was often conceptualized. It could be used as a vehicle to promote change. At that point, however, the issues of labor unionism and socialism were volatile enough that Horsley and Sinclair found funding difficult, and their ambitious production endeavor eventually failed.

Horsley's idealistic concept of film, of course, did not emerge in a vacuum. It was a response to that early period in film history in which the boundaries of who made movies—and for what reasons—had been fairly fluid. Sinclair had already made a film of *The Jungle* in

1913. The National Child Labor Committee had endorsed melo-dramas exposing the exploitation of young laborers in the pre-World War I era. In the earlier years of the film industry, the labor movement had been treated from a broad spectrum of ideological perspectives. Like the films on tenement dwellers or political corruption, the motion pictures about labor drew their subject matter from the nation's headlines. The labor movement affected virtually all elements of American society—including workers in the film industry itself.

During a leisurely showing of films in a Chicago theater in October of 1914, a stink bomb suddenly exploded, its fumes sending the audience scattering for exits. Projectionists and theater employees, disgruntled by the low wages doled out to them by theater owners, had struck back against their employers in a fashion that had increasingly become a measure of labor unrest. Such acts of protest were not unusual on the part of workers. During the same week in Chicago, independent taxi drivers had instantly evacuated a hotel when their stink bomb missed a targeted company-run taxi and landed in the middle of a hotel lobby. The growing dispute between "labor versus capital"—as the Edison film had put it in 1910—erupted at times into full-scale warfare. Walk-outs, strikes, and sabotage became the most potent weapon wielded by many workers, including, on occasion, those within the entertainment industry itself. Theater employees, struggling to unionize, brought the battle directly into the movie houses of 1914.

It was an ironic action: it could have stepped directly off the movie screen. The very movies that the striking projectionists fed into their machines often dramatized similar actions that fictionalized the events. The relationship between entertainment—the world created in films—and reality—the world created in city streets, factories, mines, even inside movie theaters—was a fluid one, the one constantly feeding and influencing the other. In the months just prior to the Chicago stink bomb incident, there had been a virtual explosion of labor films. *The Struggle* (1913), *The Riot* (1913), *The Strike Leader* (1913), *The Great Mine Disaster* (1914), *Why?* (1913), *The Strike at Coaldale* (1914), and *Rags to Riches* (1913), among many others, adapted the volatile issues of the labor union movement to the movie screen.

So common were the dramas of strikes and riots that the distributing company, General Films, promoted the Lubin Company's conservative melodrama, *A Hero among Men,* as one of a growing collection of "labor movement stories" in 1913. Later, during the summer of that year, the distributor put together a package of films carefully advertised as a balance between politics and romance: "A crook play, a labor movement story, a film dealing with misdirected justice, and a picture of love and human interest."[3] In 1913, the "strike" films had grown so prolific that they drew the attention of the labor advocate John Graham Brooks. "As in the moving pictures before us," he observed, "are events [of the labor movement] involving on any calendar day far more bitterness than the sharp agonies of the down-going Titanic."[4] The fact that he likened the actual events to films is an indication of the new power of the cinema as the new art and entertainment form of the film drew its inspiration from the conflicts in the newspapers.

The events to which Brooks referred struck at the very heart of the nation's economic system. Workers across the country, whether in movie theaters or in factories, mines, and sweatshops, reacted against the hazardous working conditions, poor wages, and long hours that threatened them not only with sickness and accidents, but often, with early death. Labor activists like "Big Bill" Haywood, Eugene Debs, and Mother Jones openly debated syndicalism, socialism, and militant labor tactics while Samuel Gompers organized for more conservative negotiations with capitalists through the American Federation of Labor. Solutions to the labor issue filled journals and newspapers—and, increasingly, motion pictures—as the ranks of workers split between the radicalism of the International Workers of the World and the Gompers-led American Federation of Labor (AFL). The films probed into what John Graham Brooks called the "sharp agonies" of the news headlines and exorcised them in cinematic rituals of order and social integration. So common were such events that film companies could shoot actual strikes as they took place in the streets and then build fiction stories around the footage. In 1910, a band of actors, actresses, and cameramen from the Pathe Film Company mingled with strikers from an express drivers' union in New York.[5] It was an inexpensive method of securing lively film footage for melodramas. Actual occurrences on the streets might be embedded into fiction films that altered the meaning of the original event. The cameras blended fact and fiction, transforming history into entertainment.

One of the earliest films dealing with the uprising of workers simply exposed the labor-capital clash in a plotless scenario. *The Coal Heavers,* made in 1904 by American Mutoscope and Biograph, capitalized on the news made by the violent miners' strike in Colorado during the long winter of 1903–04. That strike gave birth to the International Workers of the World, led by "Big Bill" Haywood. In language that could, had American Mutoscope and Biograph made a more complex film, have served dramatically as title cards for *The Coal Heavers,* Haywood eloquently waved away the possibility of simple reform. "There was no means of escaping from the gigantic force that was relentlessly crushing all of them beneath its cruel heel," he remembered in his autobiography. "The people of those dreadful mining camps were in a fever of revolt. There was no method of appeal; strike was their only weapon."[6] Yet the audiences who watched *The Coal Heavers* saw no "dreadful mining camps," no relentless "gigantic force." That "fever of revolt" of which Haywood wrote became reduced in *The Coal Heavers* to a simple portrait of miners shoveling coal onto an abusive, white-suited foreman, who fled the scene after a series of humiliations dealt out by the miners. Gleeful workers celebrated their victory by dancing about with their shovels held high over their heads, looking squarely into the stationary camera, their grins shining through faces caked with black makeup. The 1904 version of labor activism simplified the motivations of the strikers to one of revenge.

Before the early filmmakers developed narrative structures, the plotless scenarios they released were reductionist by their very nature. Yet those short scenarios, like *A Legal Hold-Up* and *The Subpoena Server,* translated social problems or fears into unreality in their own primitive fashion. *The Coal Heavers* captured the simple joy of authority overruled and ridiculed. It was a similar sort of anarchic glee that Mack Sennett popularized with his Keystone Kops some ten years later.

In the context of 1904, it was not surprising that the miners' activism should have been the subject of one of the first union films. The conflicts between miners and owners in the untamed West had captured the nation's attention with vigilante groups, violence, and frame-ups. Soon the conventions of the newly emerging western combined with the issue of labor in films that fictionalized strikes in mining communities. By 1911, the Edison Film Company was advertising its film, *Nell's Last Deal,* as "another of those thrilling coal mine pictures."[7] The mining films stepped into the territory of the western with their rough heroes, saloons, and frontier violence. Unlike the western, these films made overt commentaries on the nation's labor problems. Given the nation's headlines, *The Coal Heavers* took on a specific meaning that represented a barbed reaction to actual occurrences.

Some of the later, more commercial melodramas were so rabidly antilabor that they appalled members of the American Federation of Labor. *The Agitator* (American Films, 1912) featured the ringleader of a labor strike who was a drunkard from outside the company; *The Strikers* (Pathe, 1909) created villains out of vindictive workers bent on destruction. The strike leader in *The District Attorney's Conscience* shot down the factory owner in a drunken rage. Rex Films, in *Rags to Riches* (1913) referred to workers as "ferret-eyed" creatures and called the strikers "the lower elements of the foundries."[8] The pro-owner film *One Kind of Wireless* (1917) applauded the courage of owners who salvaged their businesses against unruly mobs. *The Right to Labor,* made by Lubin Films in 1909, championed the cause of the lone worker—the "rugged individual"—who chose to oppose the union.

Subtle messages about the value of work and the nature of patriotism itself slipped into the antiunion films. *The Right to Labor* suggested that the "true American" would buck the system of labor unionism. In its first scenes, a union agitator from out of town arrived at the steel mill and soon convinced the workers to strike for higher wages.[9] The implication was that the workers were happy until the "outside agitator" came along to disturb an efficient, amicable labor relationship. John, the hero of *The Right to Labor* and a devoted family man, refused to join their movement, swayed by the mill owner's explanation that a "depression in business" would not allow the salary raise demanded by the strikers. John remained on the job, informing his fellow workers that "this is a free country. You have the right to strike. I have the right to labor." His words implied that labor unionists sought to undermine American democracy. John crossed the picket line day after day, a solitary figure of America's brave lone hero, so celebrated by the ideal of the "self-made man." In retaliation, his former co-workers tried to dynamite his home. Thus the labor activists posed a direct threat not only to individual freedoms, but to the family and home. The would-be saboteurs failed, however, and *The Right to Labor* concluded by demonstrating that workers were rewarded if they obeyed authority. In three months, productivity at the mill had increased, the kindly boss hired back the strikers with a raise, and promoted John to supervisor. Under the guidance of wise corporate leadership, both capitalism and democracy were proven to work. Such heroes as John could work their way up the archetypal corporate ladder by remaining loyal to the company. The cinema transformed the real dilemmas faced by workers across the country into fantastic solutions that reinforced fealty to the corporate ideal and the work ethic.

The *Moving Picture World*'s reviewer saw the film as more than passing fantasy. Motion pictures, he thought, could be of use in calming the impulse to strike. A worker might recall its message should he be called upon to "decide whether he shall go with a crowd of agitators, or shall choose the conservative course and stand by his firm." Hence the Lubin film was "well worth preservation as an inspiration to conservative action when any dispute of this character arises."[10] Film, according to this reviewer, was propaganda that could prevent radical actions on the part of workers. It could serve as a mediator between real events and the public's perception of those incidents.

The critical reception given *Capital Versus Labor* in 1910 also indicated that the motion pictures were seen as potential tools for stilling the antagonisms between workers and owners. The reviewer again located the film's major value in the conservative effect it might have on labor conflict. When bloody fights between workers and company thugs erupted in the film, a minister, not a union leader, calmed the mobs. He convinced the capitalist to compromise with the workers. The film thus pointed out the futility of rioting in the streets while it still granted legitimacy to the workers' complaints. But the violent realism of *Capital Versus Labor* made the critic shudder as he wrote his review. The film was "much too realistic to be comfortable," with its mobs of rioting workers and uncontrolled violence that mirrored too graphically the stories behind the headlines. Yet the reviewer groped for a positive impact that the film might have despite its harrowing scenes. "Perhaps," he hoped, as did the reviewer of *The Right to Labor*, "the picture will have a salutary influence during this season when strikes pervade the air and from almost every section of the country comes talk of industrial complaint."[11]

The cinematic power recognized by the two critics was one that labor activists—the American Federation of Labor and Socialists alike—took even more seriously. In 1910, Chicago Socialists protested labor films that they interpreted as "attempts by manufacturers to poison people's minds." All across the country, such films showed what the Socialists called "impossible scenes of strikes" that sensationalized the workers' actual efforts to win their demands.[12] In the fall of 1910, the Washington Central Labor Union met to condemn "moving picture shows [that depict] so-called strikes, blowing up bridges, and [workers] committing other such depredations."[13] Meeting in Washington, D.C., the union members voted unanimously to protest local theaters' showing motion pictures that, like *The Right to Labor* and *Capital Versus Labor,* distorted labor activism. "Wrong impressions," they feared, "were spread among citizens generally by pictures which wrongfully represented striking workers wreaking vengeance on employers, wrecking property and committing other crimes."[14] The new entertainment form, it seemed, was capable of vastly distorting the labor situation—but not in the way that Frederick Howe had feared when he warned that film might become the "daily press" of syndicalists and Socialists. It had become, at times, propaganda for the new capitalists. The AFL soon took up the battle begun by the Central Labor Union, and found a place on its convention agenda in 1910 to speak out against the antilabor propaganda in the cinema. Meeting in St. Louis, the convention members discussed the power of the film industry to slant audiences against their cause. Delegates debated what strategies would be most effective against the moving pictures that stereotyped union members as wild-eyed radicals, lazy opportunists, or alcoholics. The International Cigarmakers' Union proposed that union members boycott such films. Delegates from across the country agreed that "for some time past there has been displayed in various localities moving pictures that pretend to represent instances that occur in so-called strikes, that are not only unwarranted, but are base miscalculations."[15]

It was clear, according to the union members, that the melodramas had been made by filmmakers who were unfriendly to the labor cause. "Their purpose," claimed one delegate at the hearings, "is to prejudice the minds of the general public against our movement."[16] Given the images of workers in *The Right to Labor* or *Capital Versus Labor,* it is clear that the accusations of the union members were at least partially correct. "It is self-evident," continued the delegates "that the scenes produced have emanated from those who are unfriendly to the cause of labor, and their purpose is to prejudice the minds of the general public against our movement by falsely and maliciously representing it by these pictures."[17]

Perhaps officials at Lubin or Rex or Reliance Films *did* oppose the demands made by labor activists, but they have left no papers behind to indicate such opinions. But while the cinematic images of the workers were, indeed, at times negative, the first intent of filmmakers was not to prejudice viewers but to win their nickels and dimes. Profit rather than propaganda was the primary purpose of the films. It is far more likely that the filmmakers simply sought profit and reached for sensational material regardless of the political position implied. Whatever the motivations, what mattered to the AFL delegates at that angry convention in 1910 was the ludicruous caricature that films often made of the union man. Led by Samuel Gompers, the members resorted to what they saw as their only recourse against the motion pictures they deemed offensive: they approved the International Cigarmakers' Union proposal of a general boycott.

Without mentioning titles, the AFL delegates left the boycott of the films to the discretion of the individual. But the presiding secretary carried the movement against the movies one step further. Obviously infuriated at the message they carried, he took the opportunity to vent some of his rage not only at the films but at the actors and audiences as well. Union members, he suggested, should also disapprove of "those actors whose mediocre ability and craving for a laugh at any cost are always attested by such expression as 'I can't do it, I'm a union man,' or 'Impossible, I belong to the Union,' horseplay that is rewarded by the momentary approval of that portion of the audience whose easily excited risibilities are evidence of an undeveloped intelligence."[18] This AFL official's indictment of actors reveals his own naivete about the actual power and position of actors and actresses working in the film industry. They were workers themselves, granted little power in those years to negotiate working conditions. Oddly enough, the official's condescending reference to the "easily excited risibilities" of moviegoers was an attitude similar to the prejudice against workers in the motion pictures he was protesting. In his attempt to dignify the workers he represented, the official denigrated other working-class people by using the same sort of stereotypes of them that he accused the films of perpetrating.

Despite the protests launched by the AFL, the antilabor films continued, with the Wobblies as the primary villains. One of their dominant themes was that the Wobblies' battles were fueled more by alcohol than by reason. In 1917, *The Courage of the Commonplace* situated a labor struggle in the rough mining country of the West, where the International Workers of the World (IWW) had fought some of its toughest battles. The film located the source of the struggle not in inequality or low wages but, as a title card put it, in "the saloon, where all trouble originated." Problems of the workplace, then, resulted from intemperate workers rather than unsafe conditions in the mines or factories. *The Courage of the Commonplace* merely followed a pattern that had already been set in the cinema by similar films. So prevalent was the image of workingmen as alcoholics that, in 1915, the AFL again attempted to intervene by publicly denouncing the movies for their portraits of intemperate workers.[19] For the AFL, both the IWW and the movies that condemned that organization hindered its labor efforts. It found itself battling not only its rival labor organization, but the cinematic caricature of it as well. The struggle that the conservative organization waged against the IWW and the movies was a difficult one, especially since the sensational tactics of the former made such rich melodramatic material for the latter.

The AFL's battle, had it been successful, would have been a gesture of cultural censorship. Ironically, Frederic Howe predicted in 1914 that the question of censorship would be raised when motion pictures began "to portray the labor struggle conditions in mine and factory."[20] Yet in 1910 those voices for control of film content had already been unsuccessfully raised — by those in the labor movement itself. Despite the outcry from the AFL, the complexities of labor unionism continued to work their way out in film.

A more effective weapon against the antilabor films was the use of the medium itself to promote unionism. Prior to David Horsley's film company for that purpose in 1918, local labor unions began to take advantage of nickelodeons to further their causes. In 1909, the Boot and Shoemakers Union in Kansas purchased a theater to show prolabor films as a fund-raising measure.[21] The year prior to that, one C. J. McMarrow traveled about the state with forty-eight slides and a prepared talk denouncing child labor, sweatshops, and convict labor. When a film critic caught his talk in Independence, he was impressed enough to promote it as "another use to which motion pictures can be put."[22] In Pennsylvania, labor unions gathered together a package of prolabor melodramas and invited the public to a free exhibition at the Lyceum Theatre.[23] But such efforts remained sporadic, and there is no indication that the unions themselves ever made their own melodramas to counter the cinematic propaganda they protested. At the time, accessibility to filmmaking was such that the labor movement might have made films had they chosen to. The suffrage movement leaders, for instance, were busily putting out their own comedies and melodramas. Reform groups like the National Committee on Child Labor, and even business organizations like the National Association of Manufacturers, made motion pictures to push for their various causes. Though the AFL leaders recognized that filmmaking might be engaged for political purposes by anyone with the necessary funds, they left that task in the hands of the film industry. The dialog on labor continued in the nation's commercial theaters, and the workers fought back with boycotts and the occasional use of a nickelodeon or theater.

The AFL's boycott was powerless to stop the motion pictures. Some of the worst cinematic images of workers were seen three years after the AFL proposals to censure the films. Released in 1913, *Rags to Riches* ranked among the most vicious antilabor films. Beginning with "the mutterings of a throng of angry steel workers," who could not grasp the fact that their company was on the verge of bankruptcy, the film presented a benevolent image of the owners. "The men will suffer," they clucked in sympathy, "but we have no alternative," they decided, other than closing the plant. On hearing the news, the strike leader turned his "narrow, ferret-like eyes" upon his fellow workers and whipped them into a frenzied mob. They attacked the superintendent so viciously that he suffered brain damage and for years thereafter he wandered about as a destitute amnesiac. Finally, he recuperated, moved from the "rags to riches" referred to in the title of the film, and rediscovered his lost family. Despite the title's implication that hard workers can be successful in America, it was the *owner* who moved from "rags to riches." The workers simply remained incorrigible, doomed by their temperament to rags rather than riches. The film blamed the character of the workers for the problems in the labor force.

In 1917, the Edison Company's *One Kind of Wireless* again reduced workers to rabble-rousing ruffians. The villain was fired from his job at the mill for alcoholism, but lurked about in hopes of stirring up trouble. A title card explained the reason behind the scowl on his face: "With a sense of having been unjustly injured, Tony revenges himself by sowing seeds of discontent among the other laborers." With his bushy moustache and unruly hair, Tony looked the part of a villain; his eyes glared from beneath dark eyebrows that threatened to overshadow his face. The stereotype of the foreign worker, Tony perhaps represented a wartime prejudice against "foreigners" — and his attempts to sabotage the company can also be interpreted as a foreign attack on the United States in the context of 1917. In *One Kind of Wireless* the workers tried to derail the train taking supplies from the mill, but the quick-thinking "Yankee ingenuity" of the owner's son, who flashed lights at the engineer, prevented them. The insidious antiunion messages of the film indicated that the labor unions' protests of earlier films never affected the production of films that sensationalized the labor movement. Films like *One Kind of Wireless* and *Rags to Riches* carried out the prophetic role that the early motion pictures had played. They resolved labor conflicts overwhelmingly with the interests of management.

The cinematic portrayal of labor unionism, however, was not a one-dimensional one. As motion pictures turned to more specific issues of child labor and women in the working forces, their plots developed a fairly consistent pattern that partially acknowledged the wrongs of the existing system and attempted to right them through moderate reforms. Thanhouser Films' *The Girl Strike Leader*, released in 1913, represented a dominant trend among the union films that featured working-class heroines. It was part of a dialog over labor activism that had emerged in the silent cinema. On the one hand, the melodramas condemned by the AFL called for restraining workers and defeating their strikes. On the other hand, films like *The Girl Strike Leader* were more sympathetic to workers, but they, too, reduced the power of the workers by romanticizing their struggles. They identified with the striking workers — particularly the women — who were so often in the era's headlines, and recognized their demands as legitimate. They addressed the serious question of workers' problems and resolved them in what had come to be known as "The American Way": negotiation and reform. Films dealing with the more specific issues of child labor, women's working conditions, mining disasters, or tragedies like those of the Shirtwaist Factory fire particularly sought resolutions to the tragedies they revealed in the workplaces.

While the antiunion film propaganda created negative images of workers, the melodramas on women in the work force carried less strident messages about unionism. The issue opened up an entire field of romantic possibilities, as well as the opportunity to place women in roles outside the domestic sphere—roles that could appeal to female audiences. Just as romance had faithfully entered the cinematic picture at the last minute to rescue women in the tenements, conflicts in the factory or shop were typically solved by marriage between working heroines and their bosses. As opposed to the passive tenement women, however, the women in the labor films were active creators of their destinies, fighting low salaries, unhealthy workplaces, and even sexual harassment.

After the long shirtwaist strike in New York in 1909 and 1910, films starring courageous, beautiful women strike leaders inundated theaters. Most typical of those films was *The Girl Strike Leader*, a melodrama that took up the cause of women workers in a less seriously reformist endeavor than the child labor films produced by the Edison Company. The plot of *The Girl Strike Leader* picked its way carefully through the political minefield it entered with its very title in 1913. Led by the "girl strike leader" Lou, the workers walked off the job when management lowered their wages. They remained on strike until near starvation forced them back into the factory. But Lou remained defiant, refusing to surrender her ideals even though her very survival was at stake. Like some fairy tale prince, the owner's son rescued her from certain starvation by marrying her.

The archetypal cinematic industrialist showed his charitable and enlightened nature once again—happily married to the now-submissive strike leader, the son restored the wages of the factory workers. It promised a "new age" in corporate capitalism, signaling the end of the old leadership and the beginning of a "paternal" relationship between capital and labor. The same theme appeared in the Selig Company's *The Living Wage,* released in 1914.[24] Similarly, *The Power of Labor,* in 1908, had conveyed a message of trust in a younger generation of factory owners. In the Selig Company's film, the factory owner's son returned from college to take over the business. In the process, he fell in love with the foreman's daughter, calmed the striking workers, and fired the dishonest superintendent responsible for the wage reduction that had caused the strike. In a fairy-tale ending, he released a document that read "Reductions made without owner's knowledge. The old scale of wages will go into effect today. I recognize the power of labor."[25] It was an idealistic restoration of faith in big business. In an appeal, perhaps, to the dreams of immigrants and working-class Americans, the Selig flyer announced that "Our picture closes with prosperity and contentment for all."[26] Apparently, it was a successful pitch. A New York exhibitor soon praised *The Power of Labor* as "another 'Captain Dreyfus' [a successful film] for attracting the public."[27] Both *The Power of Labor* and *The Girl Strike Leader* played both sides of the capital versus labor question: the workers' demands were legitimate, and the strike their only recourse. Yet it suggested that minor changes in management would transform the lives of the female workers.

Another, more subtle point was made about the nature of feisty women like Lou. It was her very bravery and her loyalty to the workers' cause that won her marriage into the upper classes. Family life rewarded the efforts of a plucky heroine like Lou by putting her in what society deemed her proper place. Women could venture outside their traditional sphere only insofar as a man finally determined those limits. Lou was allowed to be feisty as long as she surrendered her independence to romance in the end.

The fairy-tale quality of the ending disturbed one critic, who pointed out that, though the issue was current, the happy ending was inconsistent with real life. *The Girl Strike Leader*, he protested, "was one of those pictures which thrill *despite* [my emphasis] their improbability."[28] But the opinion that movies should be realistic was, of course, a naive critical view. Part of the success of films was the blending of the ordinary with the improbable to form a cinematic world that linked social conventions with psychological desires. Countless melodramas held their audiences spellbound not with realism but with the release of improbable fantasy. Such magic was the essence of cinematic problem solving, weaving fantastic solutions to the most urgent real-life problems. It was a process alluded to, finally, by the critic. Exhibitors, he felt, would do well to book the film despite its implausibility. "One cannot but feel a thrill of pleasure to see this dramatic story work out to its conclusion. Of dime novel order and all the rest, it is interesting because it represents the final triumph of sturdy human qualities."[29] Those "sturdy human qualities"—of loyalty, charity, and, finally, of love—

provided a vehicle for the film's ideological position on labor.

In contrast to the actual events of the labor movement, the films that dramatized them were "of dime novel order" indeed. They simplified complex social problems to an individual level. As Thanhouser filmed *The Girl Strike Leader*, an actual strike of women garment workers had just ended after months of hardship. The actual New York strike of women garment workers during the winter of 1910 was, according to an observer from *The Outlook*, "the biggest and most bitter strike of women in the history of American labor troubles."[30] The article profiled the courageous strike leader, a young immigrant woman who may have served as the prototype for *The Girl Strike Leader*. Though the cinema may have adapted the real characters of the movement for fictional heroines, moving pictures generally avoided the arguments that the strikers made.

The romantic endings of strike melodramas obscured the larger purpose of the issues they transformed into entertainment. When *At the Gringo Mine* settled the clash between miners and owner with a marriage between the owner's daughter and the foreman, one reviewer aptly summarized the resolution. "If not of salaries, there was a raising of hats at the Gringo Mine at news of the betrothal."[31] In singling out a beautiful heroine to represent organized working women, the films celebrated individualism and the family, forgetting the labor rights they had raised. Ruth Hanna McCormick, a wealthy suffragist (who funded her own film melodrama to promote votes for women in 1914), warned working women in 1913 that such individualism stood in the way of their movement. "The greatest argument of man against women has been that all women are individualists," she informed the Women's Trade Union League of Chicago.[32] The transformation of Thanhouser's heroine, Lou, from an active working woman to first a solitary striker and then a beautiful bride perfectly illustrates McCormick's point.

If the women strikers were not eagerly awaiting matrimony, they became cinematic shrews. Essanay Films' *The Long Strike* featured a labor leader who courted the boss's son to win the demands of the women strikers. Unlike "the girl strike leader" of the Thanhouser film, she summarily rejected him after she won her raise. Although the melodrama recognized that a working woman could want more than a husband, the alternative was a selfish creature who proved that, if given the chance, working women could be as exploitative as factory owners. Her exploitation of the boss's son made him a sympathetic character.[33] That conclusion also told audiences that, despite inequalities in the workplace, the gulf between America's economic classes was not so great as the labor strikes made it appear.

In 1912, *How the Cause Was Won* unified workers and owners. While the working-class heroine married the owner's son, her father and the owner discovered a common bond as Civil War veterans. Thus love and war, in this case, proved the commonality of all Americans, and Selig Films advertised it as an "appeal to Americanism."[34] The film cast neither strikers nor owners as villains. In the final analysis, however, the workers remained dependent on the whims of a capricious owner.[35] As false as such resolutions rang, they nonetheless reassured audiences that a day might come when such fiery confrontations as those at Lawrence, Massachusetts, or Paterson, New Jersey, where strikes ripped apart the community, could be settled nonviolently. Though those actual struggles belied the fairy-tale distortions of labor efforts in the cinema, the films minimized the clash between economic classes in America, suggesting that romance was the great leveler.

The films turned women strikers into cinematic Cinderellas. Audiences watched the actual battlefields of real-life strikes converted into a fantasy land of romance and order. The cinematic version of the clash between workers and capitalists served a purpose that consistently drew audiences: to romanticize the labor organizers was also to defuse their power. It turned the real labor issues into trivial matters that paled beside the appeal of romance.

Critics played a central role in garnering those audiences. They suggested that exhibitors select films sympathetic to both workers and owners—those films that carefully negotiated the labor conflict—for theaters in working-class districts. George Blaisdell at *Moving Picture World* is a case in point. In 1913, he recommended that Kalem's *The Struggle*, with its portrayal of brave mill workers fighting against absentee owners who allowed the workplace to become an unsafe firetrap, would "go well . . . especially in manufacturing centers; it is in the latter that the feelings of the men on the screen will be thoroughly understood."[36] More important, though, than the depiction of the struggle was its success, proving that workers could gain their rights within the dominant order. A year later, Blaisdell again suggested another film, *The Better Man*, for working-class audiences who could "naturally sympathize" with the striking heroes and heroines, and also watch the negotiation of the clash by the patient diplomacy of a clergyman, who played the title role of the film.[37] By the same reasoning, *Variety* suggested that *The Strikers,* a 1914 melodrama, would go over well in "the smaller houses, especially if they are located in manufacturing areas."[38]

At the same time, labor reformers were making films that attempted to bring their messages to wider audiences than those recommended by Blaisdell. While the commercial labor films embraced both the reactionary statements against strikers and the more subtle romantic melodramas, they also moved in another direction typical of the era—into overt calls for reform, particularly for child labor laws. That issue was one of the most emotionally charged subjects of the Progressive period. The portraits that photojournalists took of filthy children toiling away over sewing machines, bearing coal miners' picks, or operating enormous looms publicized one of the greatest wrongs of the era. Struggles to initiate laws to prevent the hiring of children under a specified age—whether sixteen for coal mining, or thirteen for factory work—grew in intensity as social workers documented the actual effects of such work on young children. Children as young as five or six might accompany their older siblings or parents to work in airless, dark factories. Members of the film industry itself debated the safety of hiring children as movie projectionists.[39] But, more importantly, the cinema aided in the documentation of child labor, both in fiction films and news reportage.

When one of the worst labor tragedies occurred at a mine in Cherry, Illinois, in 1909, it became a subject for theater exhibitors. An explosion killed over four hundred miners, including many children, and a slide show of the aftermath toured nickelodeons in much the same way that Jacob Riis had, with his photographs of the "submerged" classes within the city slums.[40] The graphic portrayal of grief-stricken relatives and dead workers drew the curious and the sensation-seeking into nickelodeons. By 1909, the simplistic message of *The Coal Heavers* had become more sophisticated, as the cinema itself developed into a more complex means of mediating and interpreting reality. With the release of the Cherry Mine Slide Show, the message of the "entertainment" took an even more complicated turn. Here was both documentation as well as entertainment. In the anguished faces of wives, parents, and friends awaiting word of the miners buried below, in the silent outbursts of emotions that audiences witnessed in the slides as rescuers brought bodies to the surface of the mine shaft, moviegoers caught a glimpse of the harsh realities that all too often became mass tragedies in the lives of the nation's miners. What the *New York Journal* had called "the futility of words" in expressing the horrors of labor conditions had become translated into a message for the eye — according to the journal, "the only door to feeling."[41] Yet the publicity for the Cherry Mine Slide Show also applauded the horrifying pictures as gripping entertainment.

Motography Magazine praised the portrait of the "pathos and heroism" of the workers as if it were fiction, but went on to point out that the Cherry Mine disaster "stands foremost in the list of horrors in America, and [has] occupied more space in the newspapers than any other news item since the Iroquois theater fire."[42] With the front pages of newspapers offering free "advertising," nickelodeon managers would do well to book the show. Regardless of what motivations induced either theaters to run the slides or moviegoers to attend, however, no one could escape the dramatic scenes without a sense of the perils inflicted on miners. The stark visual images needed no accompanying editorial.

It was that visual editorializing that inspired *Outlook Magazine* to challenge the company to justify the hiring of young boys who lost their lives in the cave-in. The photographs making their way through the nation's nickelodeons were proof of the young ages of some of the miners. They opened charges that child labor had been responsible for the accident. In the words of the *Outlook's* columnist, "if the miners who lost their lives at Cherry have called the attention of this Nation to this grave evil and have stimulated men to take action for a remedy, they have died in a great cause."[43] The slide show of that episode in labor history was instrumental in renewing calls against child labor and heightening the protest against dangerous mines. While melodramas often obscured the larger issues of labor and capital, the "Cherry Mine Show" revealed that the cinema could act as an important forum and catalyst for change.

That function of film as a powerful agent for change instigated the making of several melodramas about child labor. It was already a well-publicized issue. Muckraking journals scandalized the country when they published first-hand accounts of the conditions that children faced daily in factories, mills, and mines. The labor union activist and socialist John Spargo initiated a series of investigations when he published *The Bitter Cry of the Children* in 1906.[44] A few years later, Rheta Childe Dorr's articles on child labor for *Hampton's Magazine* again forced the issue to national attention.[45] The reformist Mrs. John Van Voorst traveled around the South gathering material on how badly industries in that region exploited children, and she collected her stories in *The Cry of the Children* in 1908.[46] The poet Edwin Markham, famous for his celebration of the American working man with his poem "The Man With the Hoe," compiled his own reports on child labor for *Cosmopolitan* in a collection he dramatically titled *Children in Bondage*.[47] Sounding very much like some melodramatic villain, one factory owner whom Markham quoted boasted that the child workers he employed were "just like cattle." He marveled at the endurance of their small bodies. "It's wonderful how they do it . . . if you just let them know you have work for them, everyone will tumble out of bed, and without washing or eating they'll be at the plant in a jiffy."[48] Apparently, it never occurred to the owner that his young employees' haste could have been instigated by a fundamental survival instinct. It was the sort of attitude that inspired a series of protest melodramas.

The Edison Company took the lead in the dramatization of child labor. The company was responsible for two melodramas released between 1912 and 1915, at the height of controversy over child labor legislation. *Children Who Labour* and *Children of Eve* both raised the issues of their titles with similar arguments. When the cinema "adopted" the child laborers for entertainment, the ensuing films turned them into waifs who won the hearts of ruthless employers. Unlike the films that thrilled audiences with mobs of fist-swinging male strikers, this situation called for a different sort of treatment altogether. The approach was a sentimental one that also urged reform. It was an irresistible formula to the organizations that tried to lobby for change. Through melodramas, the National Child Labor Committee hoped to enlarge its network of support. In 1912, it joined the growing numbers of reformers who sought out the Edison Company for help in promoting their ideas.

Children Who Labour resulted from the collaboration. It avoided questions about the larger economic system while it made an eloquent case for the liberation of children from the nation's factories and mills. Beginning with a sweeping scene of children trudging in the early morning to the mill where they spent their daylight hours, the melodrama focused on the dilemma of an immigrant who was unable to find work. Faced with starvation, he sent his own daughter to work for a factory owner who hired only youngsters as cheap labor. A twist of fate, however, reversed the roles of the rich industrialist and the new immigrant in a bizarre series of events. When the mill owner became separated from his daughter on a train trip through the country, the foreigner adopted the lost child and put her to work in a mill owned by her own family.

When she was discovered by her father, she insisted that wages must be raised for adult workers so that their children would not have to work. Though *Children Who Labour* ended happily, the last title card reminded audiences that the situation was serious. "The condition called 'child labor,' " it read, "still exists and demands our attention." The simple solution that the melodrama offered would not work in real life, and the film attempted to insert an overt call for change into a typical cinematic formula for entertainment.

The Thanhouser Company repeated the effort in a year when it released *The Cry of the Children,* taking its title directly from Mrs. John Van Voorst's collection of articles. While Van Voorst cited specific details, named communities, pointed an accusing finger at individuals, and compiled statistics on child laborers in textile mills, the Thanhouser Company's melodrama attempted to engrave images more deeply on the heart than the mind. Van Voorst documented the children's faces in vivid terms—she described them as "faded masks of withered flesh"[49]—and the moving picture dramas animated those images in a way that transformed her findings into a question of the personal greed of factory owners.

In a longer, more complicated tale than that of *Children Who Labour,* the melodrama used all the cinematic icons of poverty to tell its tale of a poverty-stricken couple who were forced to bring their children to work alongside them in a mill. The bare floors and windows, straightbacked chair, sagging cot, half-burned candle and tattered shawl had come to signify a tragic story to follow, as the melodramatic conventions became predictable.

Parallel editing allowed the audience to compare the factory owner and his wife with the mill family. The "boss" puffed a cigarette and read the newspaper while his maid served him coffee. His wife, draped in a fur, leisurely stretched out on a sofa. The film objectified her into an icon of wealth. In contrast, the film cut to the workers beginning their day at the factory in tattered clothes. Such editing allowed the early cinema to build its drama with a crude dialectic. Camera cutting provided an immediate sense of contradiction, an almost instinctive dialectic between what D. W. Griffith called "the two halves." Their resolution was both ideological and emotional.

In an ideological sense, *The Cry of the Children* avoided the questions raised by the era's Socialists. Its heroes and heroines simply wanted better treatment within the existing economic system. The film responded to the portraits of gun-happy strikers of earlier films, and revealed workers as reasonable men and women whose demands were legitimate. They declared a strike only after first asking the owner for a raise. Their strike was without the violence that characterized so many other labor movement films, and the workers remained dignified through months of a strike that finally collapsed. A scene of "The Victors"—as a title card phrased it—revealed the owner celebrating in his home with a party. Women in satin and men in top hats gathered to toast what a second title card called "the return of productivity." Though *The Cry of the Children* avoided raising socialism as an alternative, the message of such visual images was nevertheless almost Marxian in its implication that the owners of the means of production enjoyed their wealth by virtually enslaving the workers.

That ideology was dramatized emotionally in the story of the leading family. Their youngest daughter, Alice, had to go to work when her mother collapsed with tuberculosis. After weeks on the assembly line, Alice turned in despair to the owner and his wife, who had once tried to adopt her. But her charms had faded. Dark rings surrounded her eyes, and her cheeks had grown hollow. "Changed by want and toil," the title card commented, "little Alice is no longer desired," implying that people were merely commodities to the owner and his wife. The wife waved her away and continued to caress the poodle her husband had given her in substitute for a child. The beads in her carefully styled hair sparkled in contrast to Alice's filthy dress. The oppositions of poverty and wealth, of work and leisure, which had been heightened by the camera's cross-cutting earlier in the film, were now presented together in the same frame, heightening the imminence of their resolution.

In typical melodramatic style, Alice fell dead on the assembly line the following day, and the audience soon saw that even the cemetery was company owned, lined with headstones of workers. The guilt over Alice's death hung heavily on the couple, and even the wife's poodle offered no consolation now. Like so many of their wealthy counterparts in the early cinema, they resolved to mend their ways. *The Cry of the Children* ended without showing reform of labor laws. Its resolution privileged the emotional over the ideological, or the personal change of the owners over structural change. Other "Alices," implied the film, awaited the same fate. Like *Children Who Labour,* it emphasized the reforms — of both human nature and institutions — still needed.

The child labor films delivered powerful pleas for legislation to curtail the exploitation of the country's young people. Film had come a long way, both artistically and ideologically, in the eight years since *The Coal Heavers'* one-reel rebellion against authority. More complex melodramatic plots allowed the introduction of sophisticated political material, and the Edison Company continued its "editorials" against child labor in *The Children of Eve* three years later in 1915. By pushing for child labor laws, the commercial cinema joined a middle-class movement that was acceptable and even fashionable. Thus the film industry defined its own interests as respectably bourgeois rather than those of the working classes.

The Edison Company took on sexual as well as economic issues in *The Children of Eve.* Like Alice in *Children Who Labour,* Mamie in *The Children of Eve* died because of hazardous conditions in a factory. Title cards told the viewer that Mamie was the illicit child of "a capitalist and calloused businessman," and an actress who had sunk "down, down, beyond redemption." When a social worker persuaded her to join his investigation into the "awful conditions in factories," Mamie surreptitiously slipped into the factory to learn for herself the extent of the children's exploitation. There, she ventured "among the oppressed," as a title card explained it, and found no fire escapes, poor ventilation, and small girls slaving away while owners "eat their fill and devise ways of slowly murdering young children." While Mamie gathered her evidence, a greater proof of the factory's hazards was rapidly building: sparks from the canning equipment ignited and crackled through the building. Soon a fire blazed through the factory, trapping Mamie with the workers. She obligingly died so that the capitalist — in this case, her own father — might realize the intolerable conditions in his factory and redeem himself.

Despite the redemption of the melodramatic villains in the films, in real life—beyond the darkened bijous where audiences watched the routines of their daily lives transformed—a harsher truth lay. In 1915, children still remained unprotected from hazardous conditions in the nation's factories, mills, and mines. The legislation that did stipulate age limits for certain types of work was easily circumvented by factory owners. Even the 1912 Triangle Shirtwaist factory fire, which killed hundreds of young girls as well as women, had not put an end to child labor. Nor had the 1909 Cherry Mine explosion, so well documented in movie houses. Instead, child labor continued to provide the cinema with poignant material for melodramas. The films couched their propaganda in individual terms that lessened the political threat of reform and added a human dimension to the statistics on child labor.

Edward A. Ross sounded a call to action that abruptly dismissed or ignored even the possibility of using such subtle forces for change. The situation, he declared, was one of virtual warfare. "Little is to be done," he insisted, "for mill children, or factory girls, or shop women, or the workers in the unwholesome trades and the dangerous occupations, or the victims of industrial accidents, save by means of legislation; but such legislation must be fought for, and it is not to be had by those who are afraid to give blows or take them."[50]

With films like *Children Who Labour* and *Children of Eve*, the cinema entered the political arena far more cautiously than did Ross. Filmmakers like the Edison Company, seeing not only politically important issues in the subject, but also the ingredients of profitable entertainment, lent their support with powerful melodramas that were acceptable to the middle classes. There was little risk involved when filmmakers pushed for an issue as publicly recognized as the need for child labor laws.

When D. W. Griffith filmed *Intolerance* in 1916, however, his version of a labor riot did take a risk with its image of embittered strikers fighting the militia. His powerful scenes of the "intolerance" of corporate owners and of an inhumane prison system are some of the most unforgettable of the labor films. They are also a reminder that the function of the cinema was by no means a simple one. Moving pictures kept the cause of labor reform alive by providing an arena for the debate over labor conditions and unionism. In so doing, they revealed the potential of the cinema to debate causes, moving as they did in the labor films from the reactionary statements protested by union members to romantic resolutions to, finally, calls for reform and serious attention to the issue.

Regardless of the hybrid nature of the labor films, they shared at least one crucial feature in their appeal for a resolution to the disorder. The issue of capital versus labor was treated as a subject demanding the immediate attention of the nation. When D. W. Griffith wove together the four stories that told the morality lesson of *Intolerance,* he implied that intolerance was the cause of suffering throughout the ages. Thus he reduced the potential threat to modern capitalism in the film's segment on contemporary America. Griffith's rendition of life in modern America was filled with labor strikes, injustices, self-righteous reformers, and crowded tenements. Griffith's crowd scenes of embittered strikers fighting the militia celebrated the people en masse as the hero—much as Eisenstein did in *Potemkin* some three decades later. Griffith forged his own way in 1916 with powerful scenes that showed the mass anger as the response of rational people to injustice and exploitation. In his version of the archetypal strike, however, the workers met a bitter defeat. The "intolerance" of corporate owners and of an inhumane prison system nearly destroyed the lives of the hero and heroine of his modern story.[51]

The power of motion pictures revealed itself in the cinema's ability to capture and resolve the infectious restlessness of the country's workers. Unlike the cinema of the urban "submerged," with its emphasis on passive endurance, labor union films led audiences through a more complex ideological maze. Sympathy for tenement waifs might be shown more readily in entertainment than support for striking workers. The subject of labor strife was a more threatening issue that could not be as easily sentimentalized — or trivialized—as that of the situation of the urban poor. Melodramas alternately cheered management, advocated negotiation with the workers, or settled disputes with romantic or religious intervention.

From *The Coal Heavers* of 1904 to *Intolerance* and *One Kind of Wireless* in 1917, the labor union films had revealed a broad range of ideologies. They had embraced the staunchly reformist child labor melodramas, the romances of the women strikers, and the violence of the western miners. They had proven the ability of the cinema to agitate for reform and explore a volatile subject with melodramatic formulas that lessened its threat. The cinema acted as a diplomat, negotiating between owners and workers and inevitably resolving the conflict in a fashion that did not require the massive changes demanded by radical labor activists. The melodrama offered reassurance to average men and women who feared both the insecurities of everyday life and the sweeping changes suggested by Socialists. With their blend of realism and fantasy, the films promised that new generations of factory owners would bring enlightened policies to make the workplace a more equitable environment. Beneath the various ideological thrusts of the films, however, lay a fundamental process — that of ensuring the perpetuation of the order that could integrate slow change with existing values and defuse the powerful movements of striking workers through entertainment.

This was the milieu in which David Horsley made arrangements with Upton Sinclair to form a labor-oriented motion picture company in the fall of 1918. Motive Motion Pictures would be devoted to "the production of pictures in the interest of organized labor."[52] Horsley's intent was to use motion pictures for the promotion of his socialist ideals. The first film scheduled by the company was arranged with Railway Brotherhoods, and an advertisement for the picture featured the picture of an elephant with its foot on the head of a prone man. The caption read, "Do you want to go back to the old conditions of private ownership as shown above?"[53] Later, when that project failed, Horsley decided to make newsreels that would look like other "usual news pictures" — only they would contain messages about labor unionism, "particularly threatened strikes."[54] Having concluded that both the Socialists and Sam Gompers had failed him with a lack of support, Horsley was ready to turn to other cinematic means of gaining public support for labor. Eventually, however, the company's financial losses and its failure to secure more than verbal support from labor spelled its demise. In August of 1920, a telegram from the Motive secretary Ben Lyons to David Horsley cryptically stated "studio stopped on account no money."[55] In a period in which filmmaking demanded increasingly complicated budgets, such efforts may have been doomed from the start. The process in which feature films negotiated the conflicts of society had been firmly embedded in an earlier mainstream cinema, but the 1920s ushered in a new period in film history in which issues such as labor unionism were not presented so consistently. The old period in which labor had been a controversial element in motion pictures began to fade away.

Even during that period, the issue was never treated in the fashion envisioned by David Horsley. In 1911, Eclair Films, the producers of *Why?*, released a labor farce titled *How They Work in Cinema.* It was a film within a film: its disgruntled actors and actresses walked off the set in protest against the working conditions set by the director. As the director, however, magically manipulated the set to prove that he could function without his workers, the film made another point about the power of the cinema itself. It used its "magical" powers to manipulate the problems outside movie theaters into situations that became manageable. The story could just as well have been titled "How the Cinema Works."

CHAPTER 4

Sexual Politics:
Public Solutions to Private
Problems

Crazed by jealous love, he would kill her that her soul
may remain pure.
— *To Save Her Soul,* 1909

The early film critic Louis Reeves Harrison once suggested
that motion pictures might explore "women's broadening knowledge
and experience."[1] Writing in 1916, he was attempting to focus the
cinema on the lively debates taking place on woman's role in the
family and in the larger society. Only the year before, however, an
entire film company had been formed to do precisely that. The
American Woman Film Company was begun so that the "sex revolt
[might] be revealed in films."[2] Led by the writer May Whitney Emerson,
several wealthy Los Angeles women organized the company, signing
on the former chief director at Biograph Studios to make their movies.
Underlying all of the films, planned Emerson, would be "a continuous
history of the present revolt of women and its meaning."[3] But their
cinematic revolt was, apparently, short-lived. Like David Horsley's
Motive Motion Picture Company, the American Woman Film Company folded without carrying out its declared mission.
    The issues, however, that the women raised were already raging in
the cinema, albeit often without their feminist intent. On movie
screens across the country, debates over issues such as prostitution,
birth control, temperance, and woman suffragism were acted out
melodramatically. Such films explored the threats to the family that
Progressive reformers publicized. The melodramas revealed a broad
spectrum of fears and fantasies. Taken together, they weave a story of

the period's shifting moral codes, illustrating the desire to cling to the traditional values of the family, yet also a discontent with its sexual restraints. An important, and enduring, function of mass entertainment is illuminated in that contradiction: in exploring marriage and romance or sexuality as opposites, the films displayed the utopian fantasies of a repressed society.

The titles themselves revealed a certain discontent with or cynicism regarding the institution of marriage: *Wifey Away, Hubby at Play,* (1908), *The Wrath of a Jealous Wife* (1903), *Who's Boss of the House?* (1908), *The Henpecked Husband* (1905), *Trial Marriages* (1907)—endless lists of similar titles comically suggested that the romance celebrated in films like those starring beautiful labor heroines existed only *outside* marriage. The cinema thus made an ironic statement. Romance could solve the problems of labor unionism, class conflict, even political corruption, but when it came to family problems, romance was left behind like Cinderella's glass slipper when the coach turned into a pumpkin. Once courtship turned into marriage, romantic love proved insufficient to solve the crises brought on by alcoholic husbands, unfaithful wives, or ever-expanding families. Despite the melodramas and comedies that allowed marriage vows to indicate a "happily ever after" closure, the image of matrimony itself became a less desirable one in films *about* marriage. Cinematic marriage was riddled with insecurities and power struggles.

Thus while melodramas on labor unionism typically resolved the conflict between workers and owners with romantic closures, films dealing with threats to the family demanded more than romance to settle domestic problems. At the time, the crises faced by the family received less attention in the press than the conflicts of the public sphere. If the news about labor strikes or political graft grabbed the nation's headlines, the disturbances taking place in the private sphere were a quieter revolution. Divorce rates climbed steadily after the turn of the century, alarming church leaders and politicians alike.[4] By 1908, one in ten marriages would end in divorce; in 1906, Theodore Roosevelt was sufficiently alarmed by such statistics to request a governmental study of the nation's changing mores concerning marriage and divorce. Debates in many state legislatures questioned whether to liberalize divorce laws or make them even stricter.

Other debates searched for the source of the problem. Temperance crusaders suggested that alcoholism and a crumbling moral code were the root of the domestic crisis. But feminists such as Margaret Sanger argued that inequality within the family destroyed the foundation of marriage—and central to that inequality, they suggested, was the lack of information about birth control, which forced women into a constant cycle of childbearing. The problems rocking the institution of marriage, then, warranted more than merely romantic solutions. Even the cinematic renditions of domestic problems demonstrated that more than a concluding kiss or embrace was necessary. While the cinema suggested that public problems of labor conflict or political corruption could be solved with private romantic solutions, the private conflicts in the domestic sphere required public solutions, such as legislation dealing with temperance, birth control, or prostitution.

The melodramas about domestic problems promised that enlightened public policy could eliminate the forces that threatened the family. The temperance movement leaders claimed that alcohol caused broken marriages, and the film industry obligingly cast "demon rum" as the villain in countless melodramas. A few films went further in exploring family problems: a handful of melodramas suggested that the legalization of adequate birth control measures could improve the quality of marriages. But the most sensationalized films of all were those that exploited the phenomenon of "white slavery"—a euphemism for forced prostitution. According to the films, prostitution threatened the family both by recruiting innocent daughters for the trade, and by providing a sexual alternative to monogamy.[5]

The mysterious "white slave trade" had virtually become a national hysteria when film companies heightened the controversy with a series of melodramas. Novels, political tracts, plays, and magazine articles had already piqued the public interest in prostitution with a cast of characters who seemed to belong in melodrama. Evil white slavers (who were often racist stereotypes of the Chinese), innocent immigrant girls, drug-addicted madams, and heroic young rescuers were the stuff of the dime novel—and of the nickelodeon.

The earliest motion pictures on white slavery ignored the links that concerned reformers made between prostitution and corruption among politicians and policemen who accepted bribes to look the other way. Instead, a film like American Mutoscope and Biograph's *Decoyed* issued a warning to young girls in the city in 1904. At the same time, the film offered a titillating tale. A sadist held the attractive young heroine captive in a tenement until an observant passerby realized that something was amiss inside the building. He broke down the door and beat the slaver senseless in a scene that is both graphic and long. Such lurid accounts of white slavery were not unusual. Miles Brothers' Films *The White Slave* told a similar story in 1907; one year later, *The Fatal Hour* featured a Chinese dealer in prostitution, described by one impressionable reviewer as a "Mephistophelian, saffron-skinned varlot assisted by a stygian whelp."[6] In 1909, Selig released *Chinatown Slavery,* which promised to show the "howling heathen flee[ing] for their lives."[7] Such racist stereotypes went hand in hand with the drive for "moral purity." They implied that the disruption in America's moral fiber that prostitution represented had originated outside the country as if it were some exotic disease brought in by aliens. Such attitudes allowed moviegoers to think of America as a land of innocence that was victimized by immoral outsiders.

All of the white slave films exposed the underworld of prostitution when they liberated the slave traders' victims from their bondage. One film, *The White Slave,* which used the setting of the Old South and an octoroon as its heroine, allowed its heroine to escape her plight only through death. Such sexual subjects could be explored in the cinema only if the resolution restored traditional morality and allowed society to triumph in the end by placing the fallen woman back into the family—or by punishing her with death.

That process was implicitly religious. D. W. Griffith's melodrama, *To Save Her Soul,* turned most overtly on that Christian theme, concluding on a virtual conversion experience by the "fallen" sweetheart of a minister. When she joined a vaudeville troupe, the minister went in search of her and finally found her singing from a tabletop in a nightclub, swigging champagne from the bottle. The sight nearly drove him insane. He aimed a revolver at her head as a title card explained that "crazed by jealous love, he would kill her that her soul may remain pure." "Purity" in this case was more ambiguous than it was in *Decoyed* or *The Fatal Hour,* but the message was nonetheless clear: when women stray from their sweetheart, their parents, or their church, they begin to violate the most sanctified codes of society. *To Save Her Soul* ended with the reunited couple back in the church, where simple pleasures could outlast the fleeting glitter of show business. According to the films, marriage would restore a woman's worth even if she had flirted briefly with the temptations of the world. In an age when woman suffragists called for the right to participate in society outside the home, such films exaggerated the dangers of being an independent woman and conveyed an insidious message about the rightful place of women.

Films such as *Decoyed, The Fatal Hour,* and *To Save Her Soul* paved the way for the grandest spectacle of all in the series of white slave films. The subject exploded in the cinema in 1913, two years after the Rockefeller Commission on Vice scandalized the nation with an official report on the women drawn into prostitution. At the time, white slavery had become a national obsession. In 1910, Reginald Wright Kauffman's novel *The House of Bondage* was the literary hit of the year, going through ten printings in nearly as many months. Its story of a poor Pittsburgh schoolgirl who was forced into white slavery in New York City blamed her parents, in part, for her tragedy. To prevent such straying of children, Kauffman's novel indicated that the family must be a stronger force in the country.[8] The portrayal of prostitution in *The House of Bondage,* however, also implied that America's class system was at fault, since poor, working-class girls were most vulnerable to white slavers. Emma Goldman herself thought that Kauffman gave one of the most convincing arguments about the economic sources of prostitution. Yet despite the novel's serious implications about inequality among social classes or problems in the American family, the greatest source of the book's popularity lay in its voyeuristic peek at a sexual taboo—all comfortably within the guise of education and reform.

It was this sort of phenomenal popularity of the subject that filmmakers began to exploit in earnest in 1913, as national hysteria about white slavery reached its peak. In that year, two of the best filmmakers at Universal Studios, George Loane Tucker and Walter McNamara, decided to make a melodrama based on the Rockefeller Commission's report. During the summer months of 1913, Tucker and McNamara managed to complete the sensational film, which they called *A Traffic in Souls.* Their gamble with controversial filmmaking paid off. The film struck the right balance between an educational message and a titillating plot that became the most successful—and the most controversial—film of the year.

A Traffic in Souls featured two young sisters who worked in a candy store to support their invalid father. A gang of white slavers, led by a prominent businessman, abducted the younger sister, underestimating the ingenuity of the older girl. She tracked down the villains and recorded their voices on the newly invented dictaphone for the police. The arrest of the leader, a respected member of the community, shocked the entire town.[9] The six reels of A *Traffic in Souls* — a long film for its day — stirred enough controversy to indicate that it disappointed no one seeking an entertaining evening at the movies. Critics and many reformers praised the film for its fast pace and social message. One critic correctly recognized that "bitter antagonism" would follow in the wake of the film, but believed that if it would "help to preserve to society any one of the fifty thousand girls who disappear every year; if it tends to make more difficult the vocation of unspeakable traders, then indeed will there have been substantial excuse for the making of this melodrama of today."[10]

Suffragists joined the critic to endorse the film for exposing the blatant exploitation of women. Mrs. O. H. P. Belmont and Harriet Stanton Blatch both commended it. They were supported by other voices who rose to defend the cinema as a means of spurring on social change. An editor at *The Outlook,* for instance, after admitting that certain portions of A *Traffic In Souls* were "objectionable," argued that the film's larger power to move viewers to reform far outweighed its sensationalism. The initial motives of moviegoers, believed the editor, did not affect the impact of A *Traffic in Souls,* since audiences "could hardly leave the theatre save with a heightened disgust for the horror necessarily attendant upon the continued existence of the social evil, and a determination to help, if only by thought and word, in the fight for extinction."[11]

But others grew alarmed at what they saw as merely "excuses" for the lurid content of the film. Their outcry is indicative of the climate building toward increased censorship of motion pictures in average American towns. In Mason City, Iowa, the secretary of the Young Men's Christian Association expressed disgust at the numbers of people lining up to see A *Traffic In Souls* in his town. Prostitution, he believed, was a phenomenon of big cities, and the film's message would therefore be lost on local people. The curiosity of the Mason City citizenry was, he claimed, a "morbid, demoralizing interest" in the subject. He likened white slave films to "a poisoned arrow out of the camp of the enemy which finds [as] its mark our moral integrity."[12] It was precisely this belief that middle-class society was under fire by the "immoral" elements represented in the cinema that led to a push for censorship. Such calls for censorship were heightened by the very success of the film across America—in Mason City, Iowa, as well as New York City.

A Traffic in Souls was a financial bonanza for Universal Films. Tucker and McNamara had invested only a little over $5,000 during their shooting, but the profits exceeded $450,000, making it a phenomenally successful motion picture of its era.[13] In New York, twenty theaters ran the film simultaneously. It was enough to ensure that rival film companies would attempt to cash in on the success. A virtual series of white slavery films began to appear.

From *The Inside of the White Slave Traffic* in 1914, audiences learned that prostitution was a major problem that threatened the country, and the melodrama's stated purpose was "to teach a great moral lesson."[14] The same year, Upton Sinclair adapted a screenplay from a Eugene Brieux drama, *Damaged Goods,* that told the story of how syphilis destroyed the family of a well-to-do hero who had once visited a prostitute. At least one showing of *Damaged Goods* featured a white-coated physician who appeared after the film to lecture on venereal disease.[15] The blending of medical information and entertainment proved successful. *Damaged Goods* reaped $600,000 in profits.[16] In still other films, *The Governor's Boss* and *The Governor's Ghost,* audiences saw prostitution affecting the most respectable circles of society.

White slavery assumed mythical proportions that reached across urban boundaries into towns like Mason City. With their allusions to opium dens and orgies, the films captured the fantasies of a sexually repressed nation. Even their warnings about the imminent danger of white slavery were titillating, suggesting that everyday, middle-class life could give way at any moment and cast average Americans into an unfathomable morass of sexual anarchy. As one critic put it, *A Traffic in Souls* was about "an evil [which] has grown like dank grass and sucked in its victims much like the bogs with their deceptive covering of pleasing and inviting green."[17] According to the publicity, the threat of white slavery or prostitution lurked on every corner, in the candy stores of *A Traffic in Souls,* in the Pittsburgh neighborhood streets of *The House of Bondage,* in an upper class home in *Damaged Goods.* It was a potential threat in anyone's life—and sexual abductions might occur anywhere, even in the movie theaters themselves. Anna Howard Shaw, the president of the National American Woman Suffrage Association, accused the movie theaters of providing what she called "recruiting stations of vice."[18] Shaw suggested that managers put a policewoman at the door of their theaters and one inside as well. In Chicago alone, she charged, "twenty-three girls in one month were lured from a moving picture show and shipped to Texas for immoral purposes."[19] Ironically for Shaw, however, such arguments about the constant danger young women faced implied that it was all the more important that women be protected by rigidly defined roles.

The popularity of the films lay less in their purported educational content than in their portrait of the rupturing of ordinary life and the conventions of mundanity—conventions that could easily disintegrate into mystery and sexuality. Horrible as the consequences might be, the notion that at any moment everyday life could be shattered in a single brush with a drug-bearing white slaver was a titillating one. Filmmakers had it both ways in the white slave melodramas. They tapped an intricate psychological process, exploiting repressed sexuality while ultimately calling for the shoring up of conventional values and roles. The films entered the public mind by both tumbling institutions and sexual codes and then reassuring viewers of their own moral superiority by claiming that the films were "educational" for young girls.

Finally, however, the fascination with white slavery began to wane. The issue of prostitution had received serious attention by politicians and by activists as diverse as Jane Addams, Mrs. Cornelius Vanderbilt, Emmeline Pankhurst, and Emma Goldman, who argued that "the economic and social inferiority of women is responsible for prostitution."[20] One effect, however, of the deluge of fictional material was that white slavery began to appear ludicrous. "How far is this ridiculous delusion to go?" asked an editor at the *New York World,* who scoffed at the idea that any young woman or girl could succumb to the drugs of a white slaver.[21] A *Current Opinion* journalist called the phrase itself a mere "catchword" and relegated it to the realm of "hysteria" and "popular gullibility."[22] The films on the subject, the writer explained, were "attractions which crowd theatres and have become the source of substantial revenue to theatrical managers. It seems evident that the idea of white slavery is not only strongly established in the popular mind, but is one in which the public revels."[23] Filmmakers also began to parody the white slave panic, even releasing spoofs of their earlier melodramas. In 1914, *Traffickers in Soles* parodied the popular melodrama; *Damaged: No Goods* was a lighthearted jab at *Damaged Goods.* The mass hysteria began to wane with the onset of World War I as the nation turned to more important troubles. The satires reveal a new levity on what had been a national furor, and they ushered in a sense of modern disengagement from the Victorian "preachments" of the earlier films.

While the cinematic craze for white slavery declined, another issue of sexual politics rose in momentum and created even more controversy when it became the subject of several motion pictures. Three melodramas on birth control emerged between 1916 and 1917. They reveal conflicts between the conservative, Victorian mores of the period and what the activist Margaret Sanger called the revolt of women against "biological slavery."[24] Sanger, who coined the term *birth control,* led the fight to repeal the laws preventing the dissemination of information about contraceptives. On a practical level, the laws meant that typically only the nation's privileged and educated classes might have access to the information through a sympathetic private physician—an economic luxury for those most in need of birth control. For Sanger, a registered nurse and a radical Socialist, the issue was one that involved class struggle as well as sexual politics.

When Sanger released a film about the movement for legalizing contraception, titled simply *Birth Control,* she wove together her own autobiography with arguments for the cause. Her own dramatic efforts at publicizing the need to allow women control over their bodies had already captured headlines. Circulating among the era's Socialist groups and "free thinkers," Sanger began her crusade for birth control in 1913 with the publication of *The Woman Rebel,* a journal that printed information on contraceptives. She immediately ran into legal difficulties. Under the broad "Comstock Laws," enacted by Congress in 1873 to prohibit the mailing of "obscene, lewd, or lascivious" material, the post office refused to mail out *The Woman Rebel,* touching off the first of many legal battles for Sanger. One of the most trying episodes in her career as a political activist—and the inspiration for her motion picture—came in 1916, when she served a jail sentence for publishing ostensibly obscene information on birth control in *The Woman Rebel.* Such censorship increasingly threatened the advocates of birth control. In that year, Emma Goldman also served a fifteen-day jail sentence for delivering a speech on the subject.

In an effort to fight the laws that criminalized her activities, Sanger turned to film to publicize her cause in much the same way that reformers had done with other issues. While in jail she had decided that her first project upon her release would be the making of a film melodrama and the publication of a new journal. Through melodrama she could both create a new image of herself as an advocate for working-class women, and make an emotional as well as a reasoned case for birth control. The avant-garde circles of Greenwich Village in which Sanger traveled with her husband, William, recognized drama as a useful tool for protest and social change. John Reed, one of Sanger's friends, had staged a play to dramatize labor union struggles in New Jersey earlier, and it is possible that Sanger adopted Reed's idea when she turned to entertainment as a means of propaganda.[25]

Though she claimed to have "lost faith" in her acting abilities, Sanger played herself in the film to counter the media stereotype of her. Audiences who might have expected a wild-eyed proponent of free love saw instead a portrait of calm, efficient, and compassionate femininity. Though Sanger had once defined "a women's duty" as "to look the world in the face with a go-to-hell look in the eyes," she modified that task in her film.[26] One critic enthusiastically described her as a "placid, clear-eyed, rather young and certainly attractive propagandist that [sic] swayed crowds at her meetings and defied the police both before and after her incarceration."[27] In a pretelevision age, such uses of films provided a means for public figures to present their personalities before the masses of moviegoers.

While Sanger's film capitalized on her status as a celebrity in a way that precursed television, *Birth Control* was far more than a revised self-portrait of its star. In it, Sanger exposed what she called "the grim and woeful life of the East Side" in New York City. She called attention to the urgent need for birth control. The film juxtaposed large working-class families with smaller upper-class families in which the parents had access to information on birth control. Birth control, as Sanger had witnessed in the city ghettoes, was essentially a class issue. Among the poor, Sanger had seen young mothers barely able to feed and clothe their children but lacking in knowledge of how to avoid bringing even more babies into the family.

The melodrama carefully defused its potentially threatening ideas about class inequality in America by paying homage to the sanctity of the family and to the traditional role of women. In doing so, Sanger hoped to both avoid censors and bring in a broad audience. Laying aside her more controversial beliefs while the cameras rolled, she took on the role of what one reviewer called "the feminine keeper of public morals"—certainly a popular stereotype for female activists in the Progressive era.[28]

Realizing that her film ran the risk of censorship, Sanger devised alternative packaging to market it in case the title *Birth Control* should prove too provocative in some areas. Two different sets of advertising were sent out, one with the original title and another labeling the same material as *The New World,* leaving the choice to the discretion of exhibitors.[29] But the ingenious packaging was never even tested. The courts refused to allow the film to be shown under any title.

An initial court ruling handed down by New York License Commissioner George Bell held not that the film would promote free sex, as many critics feared, but rather that the contrast between working- and upper-class families would "have a tendency to promote class hatred."[30] Similar to Frederic Howe's statement on motion picture censorship some three years earlier, Bell's objection was primarily to the film's political ideology rather than to the moral issues it raised.

Always prepared for a battle, Sanger fought back against the legal authorities with shrewdly mustered forces. Ironically, she sought out the support of the upper classes to oppose the ruling. She had observed that "a few women of wealth but of liberal tendencies had been actively concerned in the [birth control] movement, but now some who were prominent socially were coming to believe on principle that birth control should not be denied to the masses."[31]

With the showing of her film at stake, Sanger attempted to rally the support of those women. After Bell's ruling, she mailed out invitations for a private screening of *Birth Control* to two hundred of New York's most prominent citizens.[32] On a night early in May of 1917, an elite group gathered to screen the film that had been so sensationalized by the courts. Along with newspaper reporters came members of the wealthy and powerful strata of Manhattan society.

The private screening was a clever move on Sanger's part. She garnered nothing but praise for her melodrama, and, more importantly, circulated a petition for its release. A *Variety* headline announced that her showing was a "coup"; below it, the reviewer stated that he found "nothing immoral" whatsoever in the film.[33] Another critic praised the "great care" with which the subject was handled throughout the five reels of *Birth Control.* He suggested that "adult audiences" would enjoy its suspenseful story and moral lesson. A glimmer of hope briefly emerged for the film when New York Justice Nathan Bijur issued an order preventing the carrying out of Bell's decision.[34] The pressure from both the media and the powerful people whom Sanger had rallied behind her influenced the subsequent court decision to stay the ruling.[35] Even so, theater managers refused to book the film. Sanger cynically wrote that they were "fearful lest the breath of censure wither their profits."[36] In the final analysis, even the backing of prestigious advocates could not alter the course of censorship. The class bias of the film, ruled Bell, rendered it harmful to society.

The decision, apparently, was more a censorship of Sanger than of her film. Griffith's films, for instance, had already exposed class inequality — but within the context of sentimental melodrama. The charge of "rousing class hatred" could as easily have been made of Griffith's *A Corner in Wheat* or Edwin S. Porter's *The Kleptomaniac* — yet those films had escaped without censure. Indeed, *The Cry of the Children* or *Children Who Labour* won accolades from governmental agencies despite their depiction of gross differences between factory owners and their workers. With *Birth Control,* however, Sanger's sympathy for socialism symbolized a threat to mainstream values. Although she attempted to make her cinematic argument for birth control both rational and unthreatening, the link between class and sexual politics that Sanger represented could not be tolerated as entertainment, particularly in the 1917 wartime spirit of patriotism.

While *Birth Control* lost its court battle because of its implicitly socialist political position, two other birth control films offered a counterpoint to that reception. Lois Weber, one of Hollywood's most prolific and respected directors of the period, produced *Where Are My Children?* in 1916 and followed it with *The Hand That Rocks the Cradle* in 1917. Both films met vastly different critical responses that shed light on the inconsistencies of censorship and on what society agreed to tolerate as entertainment.

Weber had always seen her film career as an opportunity to advance her moral convictions, and birth control was only one of many social issues that she dramatized. In her own words, she "was convinced the theatrical profession needed a missionary, [and] went on the stage filled with a great desire to convert my fellowmen."[37] Her thinking sprang from a curious combination of the Progressive notion of "uplight," optimistic reformism, and a Victorian sense of religious responsibility. With her husband, Phillip Smalley, she turned out numerous motion pictures that allowed her to act as a social crusader. In a conversation with a studio journalist at Universal, Lois Weber claimed that she often found inspiration for her films in the editorial pages of newspapers. "I'll tell you just what I'd like to be," she confided,

> and that is, the editorial page of the Universal Company. My close study of the editorial page has taught me that it speaks with stentorian tones and that its effect is far reached upon thousands of readers. . . . The newspaper and the clergyman each do much good in their respective fields and I feel that like them I can, in this motion picture field, also deliver a message to the world in the plays we have in contemplation that will receive a ready and cheerful response from the better element of the big general public.[38]

James Oppenheim, the Progressive who had scripted *The Fight for Right* in 1913, also wrote scripts for Weber. Oppenheim had done settlement work and began writing scripts while he taught at the Hebrew Technical Institute.[39] Through making films with such writers as Oppenheim, Weber found, "I can preach to my heart's content."[40] And preach she did: on temperance (*Hop, the Devil's Brew*), capital punishment (*The People Versus John Doe*), religious intolerance (*Hypocrisy*), and, finally, birth control.[41]

Weber had launched her attack on the hypocrisy of the laws against birth control even before Sanger's film, with *Where Are My Children?* She approached the subject, however, with political values that were sharply in contrast to Sanger's feminism. The title itself of Weber's film reveals the values that she placed on the family and on the role of women within it, despite her own chosen career. The melodrama starred a flighty, upper-class woman who underwent repeated abortions rather than sacrifice her lively social life for motherhood. Her husband asks the question in the title when he learns that they are childless by her choice.

Although *Where Are My Children?* portrayed abortion as an act carried out by irresponsible, wealthy women, a subplot in the film made a strong case for the legalization of birth control. In a moral contrast to the childless socialite, Weber also introduced a physician in her film, who was arrested for dispensing information on contraceptives to his patients in the ghetto. Weber's message was a twofold one that merged reformism with Victorian conventions: although she exposed what she saw as an abuse of birth control, she also believed that more responsible motherhood would exist in all social classes if contraception were legalized. In a title card, the accused physician protests, "I am accused of distributing indecent literature because I advocate birth regulation. The law should help instead of hinder me." With such a blatant statement of purpose, the film ran the risk of censorship despite Weber's traditional view of the family and her condemnation of "social butterflies."

Yet *Where Are My Children?*, finally, escaped censorship. Officials at Universal Films, which released the film, had foreseen the potential for difficulties and helped stave off critics with an opening title card that explained the studio's principles in making the motion picture. The cinema should enjoy the same right, the title card claimed, as that given to the press to delve into current topics. In the 1915 *Mutual* v. *Ohio* decision, the Supreme Court had ruled that the First Amendment did not apply to motion pictures. They were "entertainment, pure and simple" to which the constitutional guarantee of freedom of speech did not apply. But with the statement that opened *Where Are My Children?*, Universal Studios issued its own opinion: "The question of birth control is now being generally discussed. All intelligent people know that birth control is a subject of serious public interest. Newspapers, magazines, and books have treated different phases of this question. Can a subject thus dealt with on the printed page be denied careful dramatization on the motion picture screen? The Universal Film Mfg. Company believes not."[42] Apparently, both the film's idealization of the family and the statement released by Universal successfully warded off the censorship that plagued Sanger's film the following year.

Thus *Where Are My Children?* circulated through the nation's movie houses in 1916 with its twofold morality lesson on the importance of having children and the necessity of birth control.[43] The film opened to reviews that took a political position on its subject matter as well as its cinematic success. The *New York Dramatic Mirror* reviewer praised Weber's treatment of the "delicate" subject. "It succeeds in making its point, in being impressive, in driving home the lesson that it seeks to teach without being offensive."[44] At the *New York American,* the critic raved that the film was "wonderfully dramatic," and a "smashing, daring subject done in a smashing, daring way." *Where Are My Children?*, wrote another critic, was "a dignified, worthy and impressive presentment of a tragedy that should be near the heart of the universe."[45] At the *Moving Picture World,* however, the reviewer criticized the film for not taking the direct approach of an Emma Goldman or a Margaret Sanger in its indictment of the ban on birth control. *Where Are My Children?*, observed this critic, grew false when it ventured away from the plight of women in the ghetto and into an attack on upper-class women who decided against motherhood.[46]

Yet it was that very double message that safeguarded the film from critics. Just as many melodramas on labor unionism ultimately avoided class conflict when they culminated in conventional messages about romance or the benevolence of factory owners, Weber celebrated the traditional values of the family. The central issue of birth control was, in many ways, an issue of the democratization of knowledge in a class society, and Weber only alluded to it in *Where Are My Children?* The title itself betrayed a sympathy for the upper-class, childless father, as well as the overburdened mother in the ghetto.

Weber's finger-shaking at an idle upper class and her Victorian morality were already losing their appeal at the box office by the following year. In 1917, soon after Margaret Sanger's release from jail, Weber made another melodrama titled *The Hand That Rocks the Cradle,* which was based closely on the activist's life. While one woman was a filmmaker entering the political arena, the other was a political activist who briefly became a filmmaker. Their paths crossed when they both used the cinema to further their causes by writing and starring in motion pictures about birth control. While Sanger's own film met praise from the press, however, at least one critic rejected what he saw as opportunistic moralizing in Weber's film, originally titled *Is a Woman a Person?*[47] The contrast between the critical reaction to the two films is an indication of the shift away from Victorian mores in the cinema in 1917.[48]

In *The Hand That Rocks the Cradle,* Weber played the wife of a physician who refused to break the law by giving out contraceptive information. When Weber's character took the issue into her own hands, she faced a jail sentence as, of course, Margaret Sanger did in real life. At the trial of Weber's character, the judge spoke lines in a title card that were attributed to an actual Judge John Stelk in Chicago on February 8, 1917:

To my mind, there is no controversy about birth control, except insofar as how and by whom it should be exercised. When a poor woman appears before me with her sickly, underfed, unwashed brood of nine children and says she does not want to take back her drunken husband because it will mean another child added to her burden in a few months, my heart and soul cry aloud for a law that will permit a doctor to tell her openly what he has told the rich woman in secret.[49]

Thus Weber made her statement about the class nature of the birth control issue, but through the mouth of an actual judge. Interestingly, however, she opened the film with a deliberate disclaimer of the class-oriented nature of Sanger's *Birth Control*. The first page of Weber's continuity script contains a title card in which the director told her audiences, "I have purposely avoided showing either the frightful conditions of the slums or those of the heights of affluence in an effort to represent my audience—the 'General Public.'"[50]

Ultimately, Weber's opening statement was ineffectual. Not only did the courts censor the film, but the critics lashed into it as well. *Variety*'s reviewer charged that it was merely an attempt "to get some quick money because of a condition."[51] The "condition" rather mysteriously referred to was, of course, Sanger's own legal predicament. But the attacks did not end with the press. License Commissioner Bell, whose ruling prevented the exhibition of *Birth Control*, also censored Weber's film for heightening the controversy over Margaret Sanger.[52] Perhaps out of an objection to Weber's self-proclaimed "preachments," the press did not defend her 1917 film. *Variety*'s critic claimed that the censorship would only lend more publicity and "added value" to it; from *Moving Picture World* came actual support for the censorship. "The family photoplay theatre . . . is not the proper place for [*The Hand That Rocks the Cradle*]," charged Edward Weitzel. The motion picture was "only two-thirds drama, the other two-thirds being either propaganda or narrative."[53] Mathematical errors aside, Weitzel failed to recognize that drama, propaganda, and narrative can be virtually inseparable elements of entertainment, even when the subject is not as inflammatory as was birth control in 1917.

Such attitudes even on the part of film critics indicate the mood toward censorship of sexual issues in 1917. Though films on birth control were a rarity in the cinema, the Pennsylvania Board of Censors singled out the subjects of "abortion, malpractice, and 'birth control'" to ban from the state's exhibitions of motion pictures.[54] But at the top of the list was "white slavery." The sensation that George Loane Tucker and Walter McNamara had initiated when they made *A Traffic in Souls* during the summer months of 1913 had created such a stir that for years afterward the issue cropped up on censors' lists of taboo topics for the movies. Even as late as 1927, a list of "Don'ts and Be Carefuls" issued by the office of Will Hayes, the president of the Motion Pictures Producers and Distributers of America, cautioned producers against stirring up the old controversy.[55]

Although both subjects—birth control and white slavery—were seen as threats to dominant sexual codes when they appeared in the cinema, in reality they reinforced those codes. The "hero" in the two clusters of films was the nuclear family. The presentation of prostitution or birth control took place within a larger context of support for the family. That context allowed a repressed society to confront volatile issues from a "safe" vantage point. Birth control, for instance, was acceptable—even desirable—as a subject for the cinema if it were presented as an alternative to abortion and childlessness. Similarly, white slavery films allowed audiences a fantastic journey into the taboo, but also allowed them to emerge from that journey knowing that "damaged goods" could be repaired, women could be rescued from slavers before their virtue was compromised, and "fallen women" restored to their pedestals. Though the films released ideas that were ordinarily suppressed, ultimately they revealed the family emerging all the stronger for the cinematic airing: prostitutes returned to their homes, syphilitic husbands repented their pasts, and childless wives mourned for babies.

The failures of society could be exposed in the cinema if the ultimate continuity or order were the prevailing message. Presenting such "ruptures" became a narrative mechanism to reveal the strength of the social fabric. Entertainment helped weave the "loose ends" —the problems such as prostitution or the birth control conflict that threatened conventional values—back into the whole.

A far more widespread threat to the family than white slavers or the "free sex" that birth control opponents feared, however, was the villain in the temperance crusade: alcoholism. The saloon became the symbol of all that could destroy peaceful family life in countless melodramas about temperance. It was an ideal subject for the melodrama, and plots spun easily from the images conjured up by the temperance movement. Barroom brawls, scorned wives, abandoned children, jobs lost to drunkenness, but eventual remorse and a vow to "lead the straight path" formed the essence of a host of moving pictures. Such conventions made alcoholism one of the most common social problems seen in the cinema. It was a far less volatile issue than either birth control or prostitution. Critics did, on occasion, object to the melodramas about temperance, but it was the films' piety and predictability that they found offensive.[56] While melodramas delivered somber sermons with Victorian and Christian overtones, satires gleefully poked fun at the temperance "do-gooders."

Both versions—the sermon and the satire—were visible early in the cinematic nickelodeons. In 1901 and 1902, *The Victims of Alcohol* and *Why Mr. Nation Wants a Divorce* animated the debates over temperance. While the earlier melodrama took serious note of the problems caused by alcoholism, the latter film satirized Carry Nation, whose mythical axe ripped apart Kansas barrooms. The parody was a single scene of the temperance leader returning home after a hard day of saloon smashing. Her own family, however, was in a shambles—which was why Mr. Nation wanted a divorce. Despite the simple plot, the message was a powerful one. According to the comedy, the temperance workers defied the "proper" place for women, bullying their weaker husbands and ignoring their children in their crusade to save the American family. Both satire and sermon, then, were actually appeals for the restoration of traditional roles within the family.

The preservation of marriage and the family was the central theme of the countless ensuing films that joined the temperance bandwagon. At Biograph, D. W. Griffith became virtually obsessed with the subject in melodramas bearing often self-explanatory titles. *A Drunkard's Reformation* (1909), *What Drink Did* (1909), *The Day After* (1909), *Effecting a Cure* (1910), *Look Not upon the Wine* (1913), and *Drink's Lure* (1913) were only a few films that warned the public not to flirt with the dangers of alcohol. Though Griffith took a solid position against the era's moral crusaders and what he saw as their self-righteous imposition of values upon the less powerful in society (he satirized them in *The Do-Gooders* in 1913), he found that the temperance melodrama was an ideal vehicle for his vision of "pure" womanhood and environmentally conditioned heroes who overcame tragedy through personal redemption.

Griffith was not alone with his obsession. Vitagraph Film's *The Honor of the Slums* was an archetypal temperance film: the hero preferred to spend his evenings at the local saloon rather than at home. His wife joined the Salvation Army to save other families from the same fate. After a barroom fight, however, the hero realized his dependence on his wife, and also joined the Salvation Army. Pathe's *Father and Drunkard* (1908) starred a Jekyl-and-Hyde figure whom alcohol transformed into a gambling addict. After the near-drowning of his son, he reunited with his family and, as a reviewer put it, "the now-sober father smashes a liquor bottle and earnestly vows never more to drink."[57] Most of the cinematic wives of alcoholics (women were rarely alcoholics in these films) were more passive than the Salvation Army heroine of *The Honor of the Slums.* With their images of women as passive victims and long-suffering martyrs, the temperance films stand in stark contrast to the cinematic labor heroines who actively fought for better lives. The two images indicate the collision of modern values with persistent Victorian codes of womanhood.

Unlike the world of accidents and redemption they portrayed, the temperance films quickly became predictable and cliché-ridden. One film, however, *The Weaker Mind,* is interesting precisely because it resisted the clichés. In it, the daughter of an alcoholic tried to entice the hero of the film back into the saloon. Like Eve with her apple, this heroine held out evil to men in the form of a bottle. Yet the film's suggestion that alcoholism was genetic, the product of heredity factors, was a deviation from the usual plots in which the blame for alcoholism fell on individual irresponsibility. The temperance melodramas, for the most part, blamed the victim of the disease of alcoholism. The melodramas continued with a timeworn formula of alcoholic father, accident, redemption, family reunion. Even as late as 1919, an adviser to would-be screenwriters found it necessary to warn against reusing the old material. "The Drunkard father, son, or brother who is brought to reform through the efforts of mother, sister, or daughter—these are already dull to all, for who had not seen them time and again?"[58] By 1919, the temperance crusade had won its national victory with the passage of the Eighteenth Amendment enacting prohibition, and the cycle of "pathetic" temperance melodramas began to fade away. But in their heyday, they had given their cinematic victims of alcohol the power to change their lives, and held out the ideal of a happy, stable family. The temperance films provided a justification for the often-criticized cinema. They preached about the family, respectability, and duty, and the film companies made sure that the message did not escape audiences. Selig Films, for instance, advertised *The Drunkard's Fate* as a "temperance masterpiece" that "teaches a great temperance lesson."[59]

Advocates of the motion pictures also suggested that the cinema was a useful weapon in the temperance crusade in yet another sense. It was a common argument that film houses were performing a valuable service by luring audiences who had previously gone to the saloon for their entertainment. The nickelodeon, then, wielded a double-edged sword in the battle against alcoholism. One film critic observed in 1908 that "it is seldom that a moving picture shows an intoxicated man that does not hold him up to ridicule. . . . The saloons in the east," he continued, "are fighting the moving picture shows, claiming they injure their business."[60]

If the nation's political and economic machinery seemed torn with conflict and corrupted with graft, labor riots, callous landlords, and greedy captains of industry, one institution, at least, stood as a symbol of hope for America's future. Fulfillment would be found not in the public arenas of the workplace, the labor meeting, or the local bar, but in the private sphere of the home and family. It is an enduring message in entertainment. Though the issues raised in the social problem film have shifted throughout the course of cinema history, the solution of romance and the family has continued to suggest individual and personal answers to public problems.

The white slavery melodramas, birth control films, and temperance plays all assured that the seemingly endangered family was safe. Though one could venture outside its boundaries—into the hands of a white slaver, for instance, or into the grip of a whiskey bottle—the structure remained secure enough to welcome back the wayward. In the very process of demonstrating the family's stability, the films acted as a sort of "safety valve" as well, allowing a vicarious experiment with a world loosened from the constraints of marriage. Although the results of that experiment would typically lead to disaster in the films, the process carried with it an often-titillating portrait under-mining—for at least a short period—the stability of the family. The characters challenged their traditional roles in a spirit of rebellion that hinted at the repression demanded by conventional values. Private frustrations erupted briefly in those scenarios in a way that, despite the enormous shifts in mores of the twentieth century, still continues in entertainment. The territory of sexual politics is publicly explored in the media, and codes of behavior are challenged and redefined or reinforced. In the body of films emerging on alcoholism, birth control, and prostitution, tradition typically reasserted itself after a glimpse at social disorder. The ultimate message of the cinema was one that reinforced moral codes—by temporarily shattering them.

A cigar-puffing capitalist ignores a worker begging for humane treatment in
Why? In the background, child laborers literally walk a treadmill.

Angry workers disrupt a banquet where capitalist "fat cats" dine with both military leaders and the clergy in *Why?*

Poster from the release of Upton Sinclair's film version of *The Jungle* in 1914, showing the beast of the industrial system crushing factory workers. (Pacific Film Archive, Berkeley, Calif.)

In D. W. Griffith's *A Corner in Wheat,* the "wheat king" literally falls to his demise, when he is suffocated by the grain in his own granary.

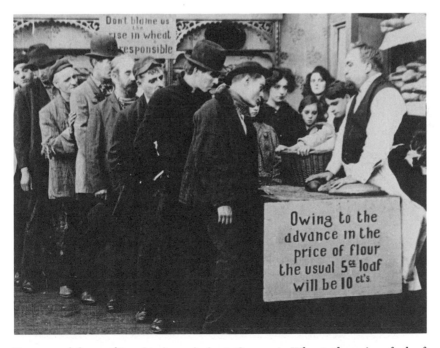

Because of the profiteering in grain in *A Corner in Wheat,* the price of a loaf of bread doubles. The sign reads: "Owing to the advance in the price of flour, the usual 5¢ loaf will be 10¢." (National Film Archive, London)

A labor leader calms his fellow strikers after a co-worker is injured in *The Struggle*.

While male colleagues encourage her, the reporter-heroine in *Her Big Story* types up a news release indicting the town's corrupt mayor who, unbeknownst to her, is also in cahoots with the owner of the newspaper for which she works.

In D. W. Griffith's *Intolerance,* angry strikers battle with the militia, and are finally rousted.

A potential white slaver entices a young shopgirl while her older sister looks on nervously in an early scene from *A Traffic in Souls*. (National Film Archive, London)

The police shoot it out with a white slaver to rescue a young girl who has been victimized by the "traffic in souls." (National Film Archive, London)

In *The Fight for Right,* the heroine urges that prison labor be abolished. The young man in the wheelchair, who had been unjustly sent to prison, was injured during such forced labor. The National Committee on Prison Labor endorsed the film.

The derelict daughter of an alcoholic in *The Weaker Mind* entices the film's hero back into a saloon. Here she competes for him with his friend, who tries to bring him back to sobriety.

The Weaker Mind's villain: "Demon Rum." It was not typical for the temperance melodramas to portray a woman as an alcoholic. *The Weaker Mind,* however, suggested that alcoholism was genetic.

Publicity brochure for Lois Weber's film, *Where Are My Children?,* a melodrama that pushed for the legalization of birth control while it condemned abortion as an alternative to pregnancy. "While daring it [the film] is not obscene," reads one of the critical excerpts used in the brochure. (Private collection, Richard Koszarski, American Museum of the Moving Image)

The heroine of Lois Weber's *The Hand That Rocks The Cradle* is prevented from giving information on birth control. (Private collection, Richard Koszarski, American Museum of the Moving Image)

Charlie Chaplin (right) plays a suffragist who terrorizes her male companion in *A Busy Day*.

The feisty suffragist played by Chaplin in *A Busy Day* is pushed from a pier by "her" male companion and, while a crowd watches in delight, she slowly drowns in the last scene.

The bewildered hero of *A Suffragette in Spite of Himself* inadvertantly smashes the windows in a newstand as he tries to evade the police. Unbeknownst to him, the sign on his back reads "Votes for Women."

Suffragists rush to the rescue of the hero in A *Suffragette in Spite of Himself,* whom they mistakenly believe is a supporter of their cause.

The hero of the Edison Company's A *Suffragette in Spite of Himself* emphatically assures the suffragists that he is not interested in votes for women.

Poster from the Frontier Company's satire *When Roaring Gulch Got Suffrage.*
(Margaret Hemck Library, Motion Picture Academy of Arts and Sciences,
Los Angeles)

Dr. Anna Howard Shaw, the president of the National American Woman Suffrage Association, plays herself in *Your Girl and Mine*. Here she addresses an audience on the subject of equal rights for women—a typical event for her in real life.

The young suffragist heroine in *Eighty Million Women Want—?* (played by the actress Ethel Jewett) converts her fiancé to the Votes for Women cause. One film critic praised the melodrama, expressing his surprise that the suffragist-star was "womanly from top to toe."

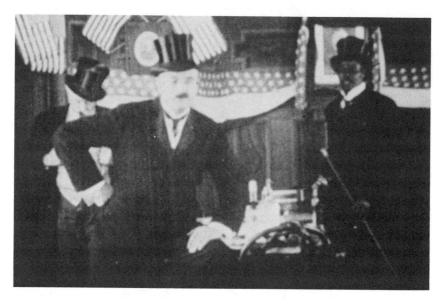

The woman suffragists who made *Eighty Million Women Want—?* suggested that corruption in male-dominated politics was linked to the fact that black men could vote while white women could not. Here, the corrupt mayor is joined by his black henchman in devising schemes to keep the city's suffragists from investigating stuffed ballot boxes.

In 1913, *Eighty Million Women Want—?* ended with the heroines, led by the actual suffragist Harriet Stanton Blatch (the daughter of Elizabeth Cady Stanton), celebrating a victory: the winning of votes for women.

CHAPTER 5 —————————————————————

Suffragettes on the Screen

Let us stop at nothing in our fight for something!
—*A Cure for Suffragettes*, 1912

As early as 1898, a short, primitive film called *The Lady Barber* caricatured a woman suffragist who commandeered a barber shop and, with the zeal of a latter-day Delilah, began snipping the hair of bewildered men. The young film industry soon discovered a wealth of entertainment material in the Votes for Women movement. After the turn of the century, comedies, melodramas, and newsreels brought the woman suffrage movement onto the nation's nickelodeon screens. As state after state refused to grant women the vote, suffragism foundered at the beginning of the twentieth century, and film satires persistently told their audiences that women belonged in the home, not in the voting booth.

Newsreels sensationalized the movement while comedies featured the antics of man-hating suffragists, bumbling husbands, and confused or neglected children. Melodramas warned of the sweeping perils of suffragism, when their film heroines ruined family life and devastated their communities. The antisuffrage films echoed the vehement cries of politicians, journalists, and preachers who feared that woman suffrage would spell the death of femininity and the family.

Like the labor leaders who resented the film satires of irresponsible workers and violent strikers, the suffragists condemned the cinematic version of their struggle. But, unlike the American Federation of Labor, the suffragists refused to let the cinematic ridicule remain unanswered. Though the first decade of the twentieth century was one of scant political gain for their cause, the suffragists waged a dogged battle that moved from churches and town meeting halls into movie houses. In 1912, 1913, and 1914, the National American Woman Suffrage Association and the Women's Political Union produced three melodramas and a comedy, all starring beautiful suffragist heroines who combined political activity with romantic and family interests. As with impeached New York Governor William Sulzer, the suffragists took their cause to the public in the form of entertainment at a time when the film industry was accessible to amateur filmmakers. The silent films they made offer a fascinating excursion into American sexual politics.

The first decade of the twentieth century was a pivotal one for both the suffrage movement and, of course, for the budding film industry. During this important era, the suffragists fought their opposition with arguments that women would usher in changes that the corrupt male political machinery resisted. Social problems of alcoholism, tenement conditions, sweatshops, urban overcrowding, disease — all the stuff of the cinema of social protest — were addressed by the suffragists, most of whom represented the educated, upper-middle class.

While Progressive leaders supported the same reforms, they differed on the issue of woman suffrage. Woodrow Wilson refused to support votes for women until the very last years of the suffrage movement; Theodore Roosevelt tepidly supported the issue in private, but did not consider it important enough to expend public energy in promoting. Suffragists found themselves working for labor and social reforms alongside Progressive politicians whose reformist politics often ended at woman suffrage, as Progressivism failed to unite the suffrage issue with wider reform. Thus, in the last years of its long history, the suffrage movement groped for new, more convincing arguments. While the suffragists pushed for reform, the cities' movie houses drew working-class audiences seeking escape from the harsh realities of urban life that suffragists sought to change.

Unfortunately, the suffragists had a far more difficult task in attracting working-class audiences to their lectures and meetings. Ruth Hanna McCormick, a national officer of the National American Woman Suffrage Association (NAWSA), remarked that suffragists spent most of their time giving speeches to each other in public.[1] Clearly, such a "strategy" would not further the movement: by 1907, eleven years had passed since any state had granted its female citizens the vote, and the movement seemed to be losing momentum under the cautious leadership of Dr. Anna Shaw, the president of the NAWSA.[2] Impatient with Shaw's conservative methods and inspired by the militant tactics of daring British suffragists, Carrie Chapman Catt and

Harriet Stanton Blatch (the daughter of one of the suffrage movement's founders, Elizabeth Cady Stanton) organized the Women's Political Union (WPU) in 1907 to bring a more spirited approach to the political movement. And when Pathe, an innovative young film industry, began a new cinematic movement with its newsreels in 1911, the suffragists became even more visible when movie cameras caught their colorful marches and demonstrations.

It was the lively British suffragists, however, like Emmeline Pankhurst and her daughters, who captured most of the camera's attention. By 1908 the suffragists in England had already realized the vast capacity for publicity held by the burgeoning film industry. When they staged an important rally in Hyde Park, the women invited a film company to document the event. This first suffrage news film appealed to a public made curious by newspaper headlines about these flamboyant women: a trade journal claimed that the film's producers had "probably never played to a bigger house" than they drew with this footage.[3] Later newsreels, eager to entertain as well as inform their audiences, publicized the movement's violence and militancy. For the first time, the public could actually watch suffragists at work, and the picture they saw was a sensational one. Newsreels like *Suffragettes Again* (Pathe, 1913), which featured firemen fighting a blaze ostensibly set by British suffragists, told American audiences firsthand of the un- controlled forces that female activists could unleash. Even the title of this newsreel seemed to sigh at the acts of these brazen women who repeatedly struck out at society. Another Pathe newsreel of 1913, *Suffragettes,* wove together footage of various British and American suffragists either marching, speaking, or being arrested. In an unclear editorial comment, however, the newsreel cut away from the parades of suffragists to young women in bathing suits, competing in a beauty contest. Perhaps the message was that here were women acting out their proper role.

The Gaumont Film Company caught one of the most sensational events of the suffrage movement when it sent a cameraman to film the British Derby in 1913. As the king's horse thundered past, Emily W. Davidson rushed onto the track and threw herself beneath the horse's hooves in a suicidal protest against women's inequality. She became an instant martyr for the cause. The unexpected suicide turned what was to have been an ordinary newsreel into a tragic display of the anguish and frustration felt by suffragists. Pathe further capitalized on the public's fascination with the suffragism. The company sent a crew to cover Davidson's funeral in detail, easing a camera slowly over the faces of solemn women marching behind the casket. Only the dramatic moments of suffragism merited newsreel coverage. Lacking the militant activities of the British within the United States, film companies settled for less incendiary subjects such as New York suffragists painting political slogans on a wall[4]—an act that the film company, in all likelihood, staged itself. The women's rational arguments were forgotten in the scramble for colorful newsreel material.

In 1912, one year after Pathe's newsreel had become a regular feature on nickelodeon programs, American women paraded down New York's Fifth Avenue and discovered film companies busily recording the event. At the time of the first suffrage parade in 1912, many conservative suffragists considered a parade to be such a radical departure from the ideals of soft-spoken, modest womanhood that they refused to participate. By 1912, however, suffragists turned out in great numbers in a spectacular, dignified procession. The film industry's keen nose for the sensational found only well-dressed, respectable-looking women calmly marching down the streets in numbers approaching ten thousand. There would be no graffiti writers or rock throwers to liven the newsreel. Footage from the film captured the suffragists cheerfully smiling and waving at the camera as they passed by, perhaps well aware of the influence wielded by the new technology. This same footage found its way into both an antisuffrage comedy, *Was He a Suffragette?* (Republic Films, 1912), and the movement's melodrama, *Votes for Women.*

The multiple use of the same footage for radically different ideological purposes belied Frederick Talbot's comment on "animated newspapers," as he called the innovative newsreels in a book he wrote in 1912. He claimed that "there is one feature in which the man with the camera holds an undisputed advantage over his confere armed with notebook and pencil. He gives a truthful pictorial account of what takes place, not the garbled product of a vivid imagination."[5] But such objective footage could tell very different stories when implanted in the context of comedy or melodrama.

Despite their fascination with the sensational or titillating aspects of suffragism, the newsreels did not have a completely negative impact on the women's movement. The films introduced suffragists to nickelodeon audiences as real people rather than the cartoon caricatures of slick magazines or slapstick comedies. Occasionally cameramen depicted the women in a sympathetic light. In a 1914 campaign report, one suffragist sounded bewildered by the attention that a newsreel crew paid her organizing efforts in Atlantic City, New Jersey. She announced that, during her meeting with the mayor, "the 'movies' took pictures of the meeting and had me pose especially for them with a great sheaf of gladiolas."[6] Even the term *movies* was new to her vocabulary. Whether the newsreels' image of suffragists was derogatory or sympathetic, suffrage became an immediate issue when it was projected on movie screens. The films might ridicule the suffrage movement in the same fashion they sometimes cast aspersions on labor unionism or temperance, but the suffragists' power, like that of striking workers, could not be denied or ignored. Unlike the workers, however, the suffragists had the clout of money and status.

It was, in part, that very status that made the suffragists vulnerable to satire. While the newsreels gave the movement dramatic publicity, antisuffrage comedies amused their audiences with authoritarian wives and emasculated husbands. With some variation, three broad themes emerged in the scores of suffrage comedies made in the pre-World War I era. The most popular formula featured militant women whose encounters with the world outside their homes soon sent them hurrying back to the safety of their families. Several comedies questioned the sexual predilection of cynical suffragists who attempted to destroy the romantic attachments of their younger, more attractive followers. It was an insidious comment on the sexuality of the movement's leaders. Throughout all of the films, anxiety over the world of the future festered beneath the themes. Louis Reeves Harrison, always a perceptive reviewer, wrote in 1911 that "the richest field for farce comedy is not the musty past or the inglorious present, but the gloriously uncertain future."[7]

In 1913, when Thomas Edison's company filmed *How They Got The Vote,* the future was indeed uncertain for the position of women in society. Capitalizing on the new vitality of both the American and British suffrage movements, the Edison Company assured audiences that, though sinister suffragists might try to ban romance from the world, ingenious young men would inevitably prevail. Set in England, the plot revolved around a love affair between the hero, a delicate-looking young man, and the giddy daughter of a suffragist leader who wore a feather boa to conceal the Votes for Women banner stretched across her chest. The surviving footage reveals the girl's mother at tea with male political leaders. The gathering was sedate and proper until she whipped off the boa to reveal her banner—her "true identity"—at which the wide-eyed men suddenly grew helpless, cowering against a wall in fear. The suffragist lectured them on "the cause," shaking her fist while they held up their trembling hands as if to fend off an evil force.

Edison's suffragist looked evil enough to inspire such fear. With an arrogant scowl, she spied on her daughter and her fiancé, finally ordering the young man away. But this hero was not so easily defeated: using supernatural powers he conveniently obtained from a magician, the man secured votes for women. In a single act, he won both the hand of his sweetheart and the gratitude of his future mother-in-law. Despite the determination of the suffragist, the efforts of a wily man were required for her to win her political goal. Even then, of course, it was only through magical intervention that *he* succeeded. The Edison film thus added a unique twist to the traditional comic themes: this time the film's happy ending included both votes for women and a salvaged romance. In this scenario, woman suffrage and romance could coexist in the world. *How They Got The Vote* managed to straddle the suffrage fence, presenting the stereotyped view of suffragists that had become popular at the box office while it reconciled the family with women's political equality. It was a pattern that later films made by the suffragists themselves would emulate.

The following year, Charlie Chaplin's *A Busy Day* held no trace of ambivalence in its caricature of a suffragist. Originally titled *A Militant Suffragette,* the film was retitled by the Keystone Company when the Pathe Company released an antisuffrage melodrama with an identical title in the same year.[8] Making his first appearance in a woman's role, Chaplin played a coarse suffragette who rescued a political cohort trying to disrupt a parade. With fist swinging and his skirt swirling above his head, Chaplin's suffragette took on the police singlehandedly, and then suddenly realized that "her" male companion had turned his attentions to a more attractive woman. Chaos broke out as a jealous Chaplin fought to win the man back. But her struggle was short-lived: her companion pushed her off a pier into the ocean. Sputtering and spewing, Chaplin's caricature slowly sank while a crowd watches from the pier. No one comes to "her" rescue. The final bubbles rising from the water's surface seemed to promise the last gasps of the votes for the women's movement—or, at least, of the angry women it ostensibly created.

The Edison Company's *A Suffragette in Spite of Himself* (1912) allowed the suffragettes to have the final word in a comedy that never took a strong political stance. When two young boys pinned a Votes for Women sign on the unsuspecting hero's back, antisuffragists taunted the confused old man. He fought them back with his cane, resisting the police when they dashed up to arrest him. Suffragettes further complicated this "comedy of errors" as they descended en masse upon the police to protect their "ally." But the bewildered gentleman assured the women in no uncertain terms that he was not interested in their cause. The disappointed suffragists watched him stagger off toward his home, where strange events continued. His maid had impishly planted a Votes for Women banner beneath his bourbon bottle, and it unfurled as he lifted the decanter for a drink he apparently much needed. His wife delivered the final indignity: suspecting him of indulging in too much whiskey, she self-righteously swept the bottle from his hand.

Again, the opportunistic Edison Company delivered a double message: the "antis" it portrayed seemed as hysterical as the suffragettes. Earlier suffrage satires, however, made a less ambiguous statement. The standard plots of such films as *When Women Win* (Lubin, 1909), *Will It Ever Come To This?* (Lubin, 1911), *For the Cause of Suffrage* (Melies, 1909), and *Was He a Suffragette?* (Republic, 1912) revealed suffragists victimizing hapless men.[9]

The most innocent "victims" of suffragism were the children in the early comedies. *A Cure for Suffragettes* (Biograph, 1912) opened with women parking baby carriages outside their suffrage meeting. While their stranded babies were left to wail in their buggies, the suffragists plotted new strategies to win the vote. "Let us stop at nothing in our fight for something!" shouted the leader, in nonsensical language that Lewis Carroll could have written. Outside, a police officer noticed the deserted children, and pulled them down to the station in a caravan of baby carriages. Benevolent policemen comforted the babies until their mothers, finally heedful of their maternal "duties," snatched their children away. Here, the officers of the law proved to be more sensitive to the children's needs than their militant mothers. Anita Loos's script left the final message ambivalent: the last title card read "but even a suffragette can be a mother." The year

after Loos made her comedy, Dorothy Gish followed in her footsteps
with an equally ambivalent comedy titled *The Suffragette Minstrels.*
In it, Gish featured woman suffragists who danced and sang in a road
show for their cause, using their short skirts and shapely legs as
enticement for votes for women. Given what other comedies of the
time implied about suffragists and their physical appearance, Gish's
close-ups of the women's legs took on a special significance; here were
attractive, young feminists using their sex appeal to win the vote.

Reviews of long-lost comedies with titles such as *A Day in the Life
of a Suffragette* (Pathe, 1908), *Oh! You Suffragette!* (American Film,
1911), and *When Women Vote* (Lubin, 1909)[10] indicate that the film
companies had stumbled upon a successful formula of "packaging"
suffragism to movie audiences. By 1913, the authors of a manual for
aspiring screenwriters could safely suggest that any good suffrage
story would go over well at the box office.[11] In these numerous
comedies, masculine-looking suffragists unleashed a tidal wave of
irrational forces that left democracy in shambles and the family
revolutionized. But, like Chaplin's character, they inevitably discovered
that cruel fates awaited them when they ventured outside their
prescribed roles. These would-be heroines often found themselves in
jail, or imperiled by such menacing threats as tramps or even spiders
during their political meetings. When *A Determined Woman* (Independent Motion Pictures, 1910) reunited its suffragette with her
family, the reviewer noted an important function of the comedies.
"Intended for a comedy," he observed, "this film is really a subtle
study of life and the influences which may be invoked to change the
apparently uncontrollable currents."[12] Against the quickening pace of
"uncontrollable currents" of suffragism, these films tucked the independent woman snugly back into her family (or, in Chaplin's case,
simply drowned her), informing their audiences that the growing
political interests of women were merely temporary whims, typical of
hysterical females. The suffragist would soon discover her inability to
handle the world outside the home, and families would emerge from
the turmoil with their patriarchal authority confirmed.
Such conclusions would not have appealed only to male viewers. In
1912, one female antisuffragist argued against the women's movement by suggesting that "our greatest strength lies in the accepted
fiction of our weakness."[13] Many women worried that suffrage would

erode their traditional sources of subtle power. When the film asserted the helplessness of women, they reassured female audiences that the qualities they used to beguile and influence their husbands were still valid. Suffrage films threatened the self-image of those women who feared that the ramifications of voting extended far beyond the ballot. The comedies, clearly, encouraged such anxiety. One woman claimed that suffrage would not only rob women of their power over the family, but it might cost them their husbands as well. In her analysis, suffragism and divorce went hand in hand as independent women sounded the death knell of the family.[14]

Comedies titillated their audiences with a fascination over sex role reversals, focusing on the deepest fears roused by the suffrage movement and soothing them with cathartic laughter. In fact, the idea that woman suffrage would produce a nation of masculine women was no joke: the comedies' sex role reversals merely reflected the thinking of such antisuffragists as Robert Afton Holland, who proclaimed in 1909 that the vote would render women "ugly and coarse." One had only to observe, he wrote, that the women were "large-handed, big-footed, flat-chested, and thin-lipped."[15] Preying on such stereotypes, the comedies presented nickelodeon customers with a thematic circus of suffrage victims and villains. Audiences saw rebellious wives hurling food at their cowering husbands, women slugging each other over election returns, suffragists forcibly dressing men in diapers, and female sheriffs pretending to hang their terrified husbands from the gallows. All of these plots were used in *Calino Marries a Suffragette* (Gaumont, 1912), *When Women Vote* (Lubin, 1907), *The Suffragettes' Revenge* (Gaumont, 1914), and *The Suffragette Sheriff* (Kalem, 1912). The world of the comedies spun about in confusion while men struggled for a steady footing in a society ruled by women. The films depicted women terrorizing men from coast to coast, from frontier towns to the streets of New York City. If the comedies were to be believed, suffragists were surging across the country, leaving in their wake dazed men wondering what had happened to their wives.

The women's movement symbolized a greater issue than political equality. It swept the ancient struggle over sexual power out of psychic closets and into the public arena. No weapon was too subversive in the ensuing battle and the comedies revealed a veritable arsenal of antisuffrage arguments. Their suffragist caricatures were irration   neglected or abused their families; they alternately represented anarchy or authoritarianism; most insidious of all, the women were unattractive man haters whose sexuality seemed to be in question.

Michael Wood has written that film points out the unconscious worries of a culture. Like dreams, the movies expose hidden anxieties and taboo subjects.[16] Without sound to make images more concrete, the silent suffrage films created a nightmarish world of psychic fears. Men became powerless before witchlike, sinister women. But the comedies exorcised fear with humor, inflating sexual tension only to explode it in laughter. Rachel Low, a British historian of silent film, noted in somewhat patronizing tones that the proliferation of suffrage comedies reflected the "hostility, hatred and fear which find their relief in jeers."[17] The image of silly suffragettes parading across nickelodeon screens allowed audiences to dismiss suffragism as a ludicruous activity of misguided, foolish women. One of the comedies' heroes, who lost his sweetheart to the suffrage cause in *The Suffragettes' Revenge,* a comedy that Gaumont Films released in 1914, stated it best: "The spectacle of the suffragettes," he announced on the title card, "would make me laugh if it did not make me cry." The two intense responses rose from the same discomfort, and comedies substituted laughter for tears.[18]

Suffragism became an increasingly emotional issue after the first decade of the twentieth century, and the films' sinister image of suffragists was a cinematic reflection of public alarm. A *New York Times* editorial of 1914 panicked over what it called "an advance in the reign of terror" created by "fiendish" women. Singling out Harriet Stanton Blatch for her "deviltries," the writer charged that her followers were "afraid of nothing; they want what they want when they want it."[19] The antisuffrage comedies and melodramas brought such hostile political rhetoric to life.

This, then, was the climate in which the National American Women Suffrage Association and the new Women's Political Union struggled to be heard sympathetically. When the suffragists answered the silent accusations of these films with melodramas of their own making, the women attested to the rising power of film. Movie screens provided suffragists with a national forum from which to appease the public's anxiety over votes for women. Between 1908 and 1914, the peak era of suffrage films, the nation's movie houses grew in numbers from approximately eight or ten thousand to fourteen thousand.[20] More than any other movement activists of the Progressive era, the suffragists attempted to use the cinema in a politically sophisticated manner. They found that the lively new entertainment form of the "photoplay" could be an exciting vehicle for their arguments—particularly because it reached into working class and, increasingly, middle-class audiences. It was with high hopes of winning new support for their cause that the movement produced its four films.

Dramatic tactics, perhaps, could succeed where rhetoric had failed. Portraying suffragists as deeply moral, attractive women who were devoted to their families or to their sweethearts, the movement's fiction films presented their heroines as sympathetic characters to audiences accustomed to seeing masculine or hysterical suffragette caricatures. The suffragists already knew the value of dramatic devices in their state campaigns. In 1911, the year preceding the first suffrage propaganda film, California had been won largely due to the use of lively pageants and plays. Among the California state campaign's subcommittees was one specifically concerned with "Dramatic Entertainments, Stereopticon Talks and Moving Pictures." The NAWSA convention report from California in 1911 announced that the subcommittee's "picture slides and stereopticon talks . . . were very effective, particularly in the outlying districts."[21]

A popular suffrage play, *How the Vote Was Won,* had proven to be an effective piece of propaganda and by 1911 suffrage groups across the country were acting out its scenes. *The Suffragist,* a weekly newspaper sponsored by Alice Paul's Congressional Union for Woman Suffrage, called the play "one of the finest arguments for suffrage ever written," and noted that it attracted many who are fond of the drama and somewhat less fond of debate."[22] The play featured a comic antisuffrage hero who reevaluated his position on women's rights when two female relatives quit their jobs and moved in with them, raising issues of women's right to work.[23]

The idea of dramatic means for spreading the woman suffrage message had caught hold and, by 1911, the suffragists had acquainted themselves with the relatively new technology of projection in their effort to entertain as well as inform audiences. A "slide and lecture show" had become a popular new device. When the Equal Franchise Society held a "Suffrage Week" in February 1911, the suffragists found that cooperative nickelodeon owners readily welcomed them into their theaters to address audiences with their slides.[24] Unaware that the suffragists had developed the slide show, a film journalist suggested that "every propagandist, suffragistic or otherwise, might achieve great results by getting his cause illustrated by means of lantern slides."[25] Only a week later, he realized with surprise that "an enthusiastic lady suffragist has captured a downtown moving picture theatre, where she is showing lantern slides and talking the virtues of suffragism to large audiences. We are not going to say whether this is a step in the right direction, but it is a straw which shows the direction of the wind."[26]

According to this writer, who shrewdly avoided entangling himself in political controversy, approximately one-third of the nation's population attended the movies every week. The "wind," as he called it, was clearly directed toward exploiting this vast audience for the suffrage cause, particularly since moviegoers at that time included many working-class men and women whose support the suffragists, for the most part, lacked.

It seemed to be a logical next step for suffragists to enter the movie-making arena: their dramatic use of plays and pageants had proven effective and they were already addressing nickelodeon audiences. Trade magazines urged the use of film for reform, of course, for an array of political concerns from political graft and temperance to labor reform. The suffragists took their suggestions to heart. In 1912 they began making films to circulate through the country's movie houses as well as for their own use in state campaigns.

In June of 1912, both the National American Women Suffrage Association and the Women's Political Union released films starring attractive, sympathetic suffragist characters to counter the stereotypes of masculine, irrational suffragettes perpetuated in the comedies. NAWSA, in conjunction with Reliance Films, produced *Votes for Women,* a melodrama contrasting reform-minded suffragists with a corrupt senator, while the Women's Political Union collaborated with American Films on *Suffrage and the Man,* a comedy satirizing a man who left his fiancée because of her belief in suffragism.

It was, perhaps, appropriate that the movement's only comedy should ridicule a man for disrupting a romance. *Suffrage and the Man* responded to the numerous comedies in which suffragists left their husbands or sweethearts. But even the suffragists' comedy cautiously played into stereotypes and conservative values. Its beautiful heroine vied with a conniving, jealous woman for her former lover, and finally won him back just as women got the vote. Romance was still the central concern of the women in *Suffrage and the Man.* An advertisement for the film displayed the happily reunited couple nestled cozily together, the heroine unmistakably identified with her Votes for Women parasol and banner.[27]

The most striking appeal to conservative moviegoers was not such overt displays of the "femininity" of suffragists, but, rather, the comedy's racist allusions to the black male voters. Explaining his support of woman suffrage, the heroine's father asked, "My butler and my bootblack may vote—why not my wife and daughter?" The implication that women should vote because "butlers and bootblacks" exercised that right also revealed the class nature of the movement. The suffragists played on the status anxieties of the average moviegoer when they presented suffragism as a "respectable" concern of the upper classes in *Suffrage and the Man.* The comedy spoke soothingly to the prejudice and fears of mainstream America to expedite the suffrage cause.[28]

Of the two films appearing in 1912, *Votes for Women* created the bigger stir, possibly because two of the nation's most prominent suffragists appeared in it: Jane Addams and Anna Howard Shaw. The initial impetus for the NAWSA film came from the film industry, not from Shaw or Addams. Reliance Films approached the two women to convince them that a movie could be a forceful argument for suffrage.[29] Jane Addams already used motion pictures at her famous Hull House in Chicago to lure children and young people away from the "degeneracy" she feared in storefront nickelodeons. At Hull House, they could watch *Cinderella* or *Uncle Tom's Cabin,* stories unthreatening to the social values she held.[30] She had decided to use film for the purposes that some churches and schools already did.

In their offer to Addams and Shaw, Reliance had, apparently, decided that both sides of the suffrage controversy could be profitable entertainment—the film company had released a suffrage parody, *Bedelia and the Suffragette,* only a few months earlier. It required a good deal of persuasion to convince Shaw and Addams to make the film. Before Addams had accepted motion pictures as an unchangeable fact of American life, she had been an ardent foe of the harmful world she felt the movies created. In 1909, she had warned that moving pictures were a "debased form of dramatic entertainment" that depicted a "primitive state of morality." Yet in only three years, she would star in *Votes for Women.*[31]

The irony of her appearance in the melodrama did not escape one reviewer, who observed that "one of the significant facts in connection with this picture is that some of the ladies who appear in it at one time were to be classed as antagonistic to the moving pictures."[32] The times were changing, though, and Addams's mind had changed along with them. She and her colleague Shaw decided that film could be fought by film; old stereotypes of suffragists could be countered with a more realistic portrayal in melodramas.

Under the direction of Hal Reid, the two reels of *Votes for Women* turned the distinguished world of the United States Senate upside down and found it crawling with political corruption. Beginning with actual suffragists—Shaw and Addams—speaking at a labor meeting, the film then moved from documentary or newsreellike action to melodrama. The heroines opposed a villainous senator who owned a disease-ridden tenement and sweatshop of the sort that Edison's film company had condemned in *The Awakening of John Bond.* Only after the women converted his fiancée to suffragism did the senator, pressured by romance, finally realize the need for reform.

The melodrama pointed to several controversial issues of the era, exposing the needs of working women, tenement dwellers, political vice, and neglected children. Left to men, the film implied, these wrongs would continue. Give the vote to women, and reforms would be enforced. *Votes for Women* established the suffragists as the upholders of far higher ideals than government officials who profited from the very conditions the women sought to correct. The theme of woman as reformer was, of course, hardly new to the movie screen. Audiences who watched *The Reform Candidate* in 1911 and *The Stronger Sex* in 1910 saw heroines exposing injustice or corruption. Though certainly not an overt call for woman suffrage, the theme of brave, moralistic women continued into 1913 with the films previously discussed on political graft. *Votes for Women* thus followed a film tradition of sorts, but its overt call for woman suffrage was unique. Its closing shots left the message unequivocal, again using the footage of the 1912 suffrage parade in New York City that *Was He A Suffragette?* had exploited for satire earlier that year. This time, of course, the context was radically different, and the *Moving Picture World* reviewer enthusiastically claimed that the parade sequence "makes a rousing finish to a picture that will undoubtedly be of great service to the advocates of women's rights all over America."[33]

The critic had made an accurate prediction. At the forty-fourth National American Woman Suffrage Association convention in late 1912, the women heralded the success of the new dramatic venture. While the American Federation of Labor simply denounced antilabor films at their conventions in 1910 and again in 1915, the suffrage organizations took up the cinematic challenge and found that "the play had been much in demand all over the country."[34] A year later, the forty-fifth NAWSA convention noted the diverse use of the film during the year's campaigns. In New Jersey, the Women's Political Union brought *Votes for Women* into the state and "secured its exhibition in many moving picture shows."[35] In the Midwest, the Des Moines, Iowa, suffrage club showed the film "in a small river front park near the bandstand where nightly concerts were given during Fair Week."[36] At the Congregational Church of Appleton, Wisconsin, a small crowd paid five cents to see *Votes for Women*.[37] Shown in nickelodeons, fairs, and even churches, the movement's first melodrama impressed the suffragists with its versatility and its ability to reach a wide audience. The film was in such demand that within two years of mass distribution, its two reels had worn out, proving that the melodrama had served an important purpose, not the least of which was to encourage the suffragists to make still more films.

Mrs. O. H. P. Belmont, a prominent society matron who had led the fight against censorship of *Traffic in Souls,* put her organizational skills and her financial backing into another suffrage film, this time using an invention by Thomas Edison—the Kinetophone. With this machine, voices could be recorded to synchronize with the image projected on screen. "Talking" pictures would allow suffragists to directly speak to audiences who otherwise never had the opportunity to hear their words.[38] Flanked by banners and posters celebrating the cause of woman suffrage, Mrs. Belmont and her colleagues at the Women's Political Union took turns delivering their speeches to a stationary camera. Edison's recording device whirred in the background, preserving their arguments for listeners across the country.

Yet it was the melodrama that had been most popular. Encouraged by the success of *Votes for Women*'s fictionalized version of women's rights, the Women's Political Union produced a second suffrage melodrama in 1913, titled *Eighty Million Women Want—?*, a reference to Rheta Childe Dorr's book, *What Eighty Million Women Want*. The

WPU, having worked with Eclair Films on *Suffrage and the Man*, turned to newly formed Unique Film Company with a plot line similar to that of *Votes for Women*. Like its predecessor, *Eighty Million Women Want — ?* featured an attractive young suffragist who reformed her sweetheart, a lawyer involved in political corruption.

Starring Emmeline Pankhurst and Harriet Stanton Blatch, who followed their more conservative colleagues Addams and Shaw onto the country's movie screens, this film depicted the staunchly moralistic suffragists waging war on the city's political boss and eventually driving him from power. Romance and politics again successfully merged in this melodrama: having destroyed the corrupt forces of the political machine, the women won suffrage and the heroine reconciled with her newly reformed lover. As the *Moving Picture World* reviewer commented, "both she and the hero look and act their best when they gaze upon the marriage license, which forms the finale of the story."[39] Like the melodramas of fiesty female labor leaders or crusaders against graft, *Eighty Million Women Want — ?* implied that political resolutions were not entirely satisfactory unless romance also settled the dilemmas of the heroine.

Ironically, an incident at the first screening of *Eighty Million Women Want — ?* provoked some of the tension that the film sought to resolve. A long delay in the arrival of the film had made the audiences restless. Harriet Stanton Blatch, accustomed to making the most of the worst situation, rose to the occasion and tried to entertain the crowd with a spontaneous speech. Unable to resist a few witty barbs, Blatch pointed out that it was a "man-driven taxi" that had failed to deliver the "man-made film" — mishaps, she smiled condescendingly, can happen even to men. Blatch's attempt at humor backfired. The last remaining men on the back row of the Bryant Theater hastily slipped out the door.[40]

A reporter sent by *Motography Magazine* to cover the event observed a stream of men slowly trickling from the theater as two hours dragged past before the film finally arrived. Sheepishly, the press men drifted out, "murmuring to themselves or to somebody else 'a previous engagement — I really can't wait' and disappear[ed] in the direction of the nearest restaurant."[41] Apparently, some nervous men found it uncomfortable to meet actual suffragists, particularly when they seemed as assertive as Blatch.

Despite the near disaster of its first showing, the reviewers who stayed to see *Eighty Million Women Want*—? praised the film, and subtly indicated their own support for the suffragists' cause. W. Stephen Bush, in his column for the *Moving Picture World*, hailed the film's exposure of political corruption. "This feature," he claimed, "gives a most attractive picture of defeat of the old and the victory of the new idea in politics." Bush continued to suggest that the melodrama would give audiences a "new idea" of suffragists: "Those who have looked upon the Votes-for-Women movement as the last refuge for old maids and cranks are due for a pleasant and agreeable disillusionment. The heroine of the story, though a stanch [sic] enough suffragette, is womanly from top to toe.[42]

Bush's use of the word *though* in the preceding comment is a telling indication of the dominant attitudes that the suffragists faced. Here, then, was one of the film's most important messages. Blatch and Pankhurst defended suffragists against stereotypes like those perpetuated by Robert Afton Holland and continued in suffrage satires. Another film critic echoed Bush's thoughts in a column that found the film "an agreeable surprise." Instead of a lecture by dogmatic suffragists, which apparently was what this critic expected, *Eighty Million Women Want*—? was "really and truly [a] a story [about] a young lawyer in love with a pretty girl."[43]

Political expediency demanded that even the most radical suffragists—and Pankhurst's militant activity in England placed her in the international front ranks of the radicals—portray their cause in a nonthreatening manner in the film, upholding rather than subverting dominant values. Again, the Women's Political Union made racist allusions to support votes for women. Scenes of the political boss's office included a black henchman, outfitted in top hat, tails, and cane, who pompously puffed on his cigar. The implication was clear: a black man held political power while white women were denied the vote. In her analysis of the suffrage movement's arguments, Aileen Kraditor has noted that the women appealed to racist impulses in their campaign for the vote, questioning a society that would grant the vote to black men but not to white women.[44] The Women's Political Union catered to both class and racial biases to expedite its cause.

Nuances, however, abounded in *Eighty Million Women Want*—?. One scene revolved around an episode in which the political boss unwittingly selected a suffragist infiltrator for his secretary over a long line of applicants because, according to the title card, he was "impressed with her appearance." The suffragists subtly conveyed a double message in that single statement: a suffragist could easily stand out in a crowd with her beauty if men were foolish enough to judge women on that basis. As it was, the suffragist/secretary led to the downfall of the political boss. This artful scene told audiences that, while suffragists were attractive women, this was an unfair standard of measuring a woman's worth—one that belonged to the mentality of corrupt politicians.

Advertisements for the film stressed the dual image of suffragists. A full-page ad in *Moving Picture World* described the plot as "showing the pernicious activity of the 'boss' opposed by a beautiful 'Suffragette' who by a clever bit of detective work, saves her lover from jail, and who causes the boss's downfall by the aid of the SUFFRAGE PARTY."[45] If the image of rebellious but lovely suffragists failed to get booking for the film, the ad continued with a pitch to commercial buyers that hailed *Eighty Million Women Want—?* as "the biggest moneygetter of a decade," and claimed that "no more advertised personages can be found today" than the film's stars, Pankhurst and Blatch.

Pankhurst was, indeed, a much "advertised personage" in 1913. Her numerous arrests piqued the public interest in this seemingly notorious woman. When the Women's Political Union released *Eighty Million Women Want—?* in November of 1913, Pankhurst traveled on the East Coast speaking to packed houses on women's rights. Among her talks was the one on white slavery that had drawn Emma Goldman and Mrs. Cornelius Vanderbilt; so crowded was the auditorium that over one thousand people had to be turned away.[46]

The mass audiences Pankhurst drew in 1913 reflected recent political gains that the suffrage movement had made. Five states granted women the vote between 1910 and 1914, a rapid acceleration of progress over the fourteen years prior to 1910, when suffrage failed to win even a single state. And, for the first time, Congress debated woman suffrage in 1913. Representatives to the NAWSA convention in November of 1913 excitedly discussed the movement's new momentum and its growing use of dramatic propaganda. One woman reported that "suffrage in graphic and dramatic form is more than ever in demand."[47] The suffragists used dramatic forums wherever they found them. At a showing of the play, *Her Own Money,* at the Belasco Theatre in early 1914, suffragists decorated the theater with colorful banners and streamers.[48] In Rhode Island, suffragists declared a "Theatre Day," when "every theatre and moving picture house is asked to present a suffrage play; to have a suffrage speaker between acts; to run a moving picture film or in some other way recognize suffrage day."[49]

Commercial interests soon noticed the lucrative potential for profit in suffragism's dramatic tactics. After the release of *Votes for Women* in 1912, NAWSA found 1913 a boom year for publicity opportunities. The convention minutes of that year noted a rise in "propositions from people outside the suffrage movement for raising sums of money by combining commercial enterprises with suffrage work." Film industrialists, for whom profit mattered far more than politics, were eager to work with suffragists at the same time that they produced an abundance of suffrage comedies. Thomas Edison, whose company produced numerous suffrage parodies, is reported to have collaborated with NAWSA to make a "talking movie picture reel" for use in suffrage campaigns. The reference, made in the convention reports of 1913, may have been to the project undertaken by Mrs. O. H. P. Belmont in that year. The shrewd Edison may have been among those first in line at the suffragists' door when dollar signs appeared in the movement propaganda.[50]

NAWSA proved so receptive to the film industry's new approaches that in 1914 the organization had two films under way at once, each unknown to the makers of the other. Both films were planned on grand scales to surpass the earlier melodramas. Noting that the Women's Political Union had just released *Eighty Million Women Want—?*, the more conventional suffragists of NAWSA competitively claimed that the association was devising "a very big ambitious moving-picture plan, partly worked out, which will quite exel [sic] any previous thing of the sort."[51] Scripting the proposed film was a task the New York suffragists put before the public in the form of a contest. Fifty dollars would be awarded to any writer who submitted the screenplay that, as the association leaders put it, "puts suffrage before the public in a popular way." To relieve any potential doubts about the film, the suffragists reassured writers that "a first class house will bring it out and well-known people of the suffrage and professional world will appear in it."[52] The film, however, was never to be made.

It is an indication of NAWSA's confused leadership and lack of communication among its branches that the New York suffragists had to abandon their ambitious plans for the film when they discovered that one of their national officers, Ruth Hanna McCormick, was close to completing another suffrage melodrama, *Your Girl and Mine.* The daughter of the United States Senator Mark Hanna, McCormick used the family money to serve the suffrage cause generously. A friend of McCormick's commented that "in addition to great physical and spiritual beauty, Ruth was frightfully rich." But the friend continued to describe a side of McCormick's personality that may have contributed to the clash within NAWSA over the two film projects. The tall dynamic suffragist, apparently, could be "selfish and domineering" as well, if the assertions were correct.[53]

McCormick collaborated with Lewis J. Selznick's World Film Company without notifying her colleagues on the East Coast. An undercurrent of frustration with NAWSA tactics surfaced in her blunt statement on the origins of *Your Girl and Mine*. "Realizing that the suffragists . . . spend most of their time talking to each other in private, I felt it was necessary to try and originate a means of really reaching the public."[54] Such statements would hardly endear her to national leadership.

Though the suffragists of 1914 had already produced three films, made a "Kinetoscope" of their lectures, compiled numerous slide shows, and frequently spoke in person before nickelodeon audiences, McCormick hinted that the movement had not yet explored the full potential of film.[55] She touted her film as the *Uncle Tom's Cabin* of the suffrage movement. Like Harriet Beecher Stowe had done in the nineteenth century, she envisioned a melodrama that would wring tears from its viewers and sway hearts to the plight of powerless women. Determined that her film would succeed, she shared power over the film with the director, Giles Warren, casting some of the actresses and actors herself and conferring daily with Warren during production.[56] McCormick's demand that she closely supervise the filming was more than a "domineering" personality trait; the suffrage elections were coming up soon in the western states, and, convinced that *Your Girl and Mine* could play an important role in the campaign, she rushed the film to completion.[57]

McCormick's first goal for the film was that it "would appeal to every man and women regardless of whether they knew anything about the suffrage movement or cared anything about it."[58] In an effort first to draw crowds and second to argue for suffrage, *Your Girl and Mine* blended lively entertainment with propaganda. The melodrama filled seven reels—quite a lengthy story for its day—with spectacular action, following the troubled marriage between a wealthy young woman and her abusive husband. When the husband used the heroine's money to buy liquor, the title card quoted his dramatic lines: "I am absolute master here," he told his wife, and continued, "under the law your money is also mine." Such an argument, of course, would mean little to working-class women, but it reflected the interests of the primarily upper-class suffragists like McCormick well.

The manipulative husband of *Your Girl and Mine* conveniently died, but the heroine discovered that her problems had just begun. The villain had maliciously bequeathed their two daughters, like pieces of furniture or stocks, to their paternal grandfather. But the heroine's Aunt Jane, a suffragist described as "the good Angel of the helpless and downtrodden," secured a court ruling and rescued the children from the clutches of their grandfather. As evil as his son, the old man had put the children to work in a cannery.[59] In the final scenes, the governor signed a bill granting women the right to vote, assuring the female half of the population that they would be able to protect their rights in the future. *Your Girl and Mine*'s happy ending repeated the conclusion of all three previous suffrage films: after women won the vote, the beautiful heroine won her suitor. This time, the star headed to the altar with the state lieutenant governor, who had converted to the suffrage cause.

Your Girl and Mine also embraced a broad spectrum of the political issues that suffragists promised they could rectify. Temperance, child labor, and the inequity of marital laws became subjects for the melodramatic rendition of woman suffrage. The victimized heroine of *Your Girl and Mine* appealed to the compassion of audiences, as she conquered a legal system that granted men total power over the lives of women and children. The film touched the early film theorist Vachel Lindsay. He praised the film's symbolic figure of the suffrage movement, a woman labeled the "Goddess of Suffrage," who entered the melodrama "at critical periods, clothed in white, solemn and royal" to point out "the moral of each situation." Like some religious figure, the "goddess" represented the higher morality of women to which the suffragists laid claim.

Lindsay noted that the character had a real-life counterpart in Jane Addams, doing "justice to that breed of woman amid the sweetness and flowers . . . of the photoplay story."[60] The suffragists understood that thorny subjects could be concealed in "sweetness and flowers," and, as far as the reviewers were concerned, their hearts were won. Struck by the beautiful suffrage "goddess," another reviewer surmised that " . . . if all suffragettes were as fair to look upon, it is safe to say that 'Votes for Women' would be a reality in every state in the Union today."61

The suffragists who chose attractive actresses to play their film counterparts recognized that physical beauty could win men's attention where arguments often threatened and failed. A *Photoplay* journalist even nominated his favorite actress for future suffrage films: William Henry wanted to see Cleo Madison in a suffrage melodrama. He claimed that "Jane Addams and other loyal suffragettes are overlooking an awfully good bet in Cleo Madison. With the lovely but militant Cleo at their head, the suffragettes could capture the vote for their sex."62 Madison herself supported votes for women, as did Mary Pickford, who risked the loss of a few fans to pose with a suffrage poster. The community of Hollywood liberally elected women to political offices. In 1913, Universal City teemed with suffragettes; so massive was suffrage support in that community that women won ten of twenty-eight positions in the municipal elections—a factor that may well have spawned a few suffrage satires. The community could boast a female chief of police, police judge, city auditor, and city assessor, among others.63

This was the creative milieu in which critics appraised *Your Girl and Mine.* Its positive reception initially suggested that attractive heroines and appeals to emotionalism could win the movement new support. When McCormick first showed her prized film in Chicago, the town's most influential and prestigious citizens filled the theater and enthusiastically applauded its title cards. The *New York Times* publicized the film's "gala opening performance" and the "unjust social conditions" it exposed.64 *Moving Picture World* claimed that *Your Girl and Mine* proved that "moving pictures . . . will accomplish more for the cause than all that eloquent tongues have done since the movement was started."65 The *New York Times* had earlier commended the film rather apologetically. "There is not too much suffrage in it," the reporter hedged.66 With such publicity, everything pointed to success for the melodrama: press coverage was thorough and positive, audiences responded strongly, and *Your Girl and Mine* was scheduled to tour the nation's commercial theaters.

Yet, despite all its publicity and expense, the suffrage movement's "Uncle Tom's Cabin" never fulfilled the high expectations that McCormick held for it. A disagreement with World Films relegated the film to private screenings. What actually occurred remains clouded in brief allusions to the quarrel. A solitary footnote in Ida Husted Harper's volume of the massive *History of Woman Suffrage* barely nodded to the film. She briefly commented that McCormick "spent a large amount of time and money on the play, hoping it would yield a good revenue to the [NAWSA], but the arrangement with the Film Corporation proved impossible and it finally had to be abandoned."[67] No further details of the schism were offered. The footnote is a sad testimony to the historical neglect given the suffrage films even at the hands of the movement's own historians. Suffrage archives reveal no additional information in the conflict between McCormick and World Films just as *Your Girl and Mine* was to begin its tour.

It must have been with great disappointment that McCormick presented her film as a gift to NAWSA in 1915 at the association's forty-sixth convention, where it was placed on the nightly entertainment program.[68] Her criticism of the movement as "suffragists talking to themselves" had become regrettably true of her own film. Though it proved to be a financial disappointment, suffragists used it in their state campaigns and it even found its way into Canada, where the Montreal Suffrage Association showed it for fund-raising and publicity.[69] The commercial failure of *Your Girl and Mine* probably discouraged the suffragists. In the single showing of the melodrama at New York's Casino Theatre, the suffragists took a big loss: ticket sales amounted to only one hundred dollars, while the advertising expenses, shipping fees, and ticket printing approached nearly four hundred dollars.[70] It was enough to discourage the making of any more films, though suffragists continued to use theaters for their slide shows.[71] The Women's Political Union also continued to use films to draw people off the streets and into their meetings. At their headquarters on New York's Fifth Avenue, the WPU began their daily programs with movies in the afternoons.[72] Frederic C. Howe, somewhat ironically, found his speech for suffrage preceded by a movie. The *New York Times* gave the free movies more attention than the talks.[73]

Along with the disappointing fate of *Your Girl and Mine,* the suffragists suffered an even greater defeat: the western suffrage elections that McCormick hoped to aid with the film ended in disaster. Only two states of seven passed the suffrage resolution. The women of Montana and Nevada won the right to vote, while North Dakota, South Dakota, Nebraska, Missouri, and Ohio still reserved that right for men only. Though McCormick's film had played no role in the elections, in her native Chicago, at least, motion pictures served an important role in the movement. There, the suffragists made the films that showed women how to register and vote, and that persuaded women to register for the spring elections of 1914.[74]

The effect of the suffrage movement's films on winning support for their cause is difficult to determine, but these films are invaluable today for the picture they paint of a society caught between Victorian mores, Progressive issues, and the impulse toward freer sex roles. The weapons wielded by both sides of the suffrage issue, like those of temperance or labor unionism, surface in the films of social protest. Myth was fought with myth, as the suffragists accepted the dominant image of women as morally superior to men and used it to their own advantage. The suffragists stepped onto the traditional "pedestal" and turned it into a soapbox from which they preached, urging that women's inherent ethical sensibilities could not be wasted solely in the family when male-run politics were rampant with corruption and interests that allowed social wrongs to continue.

The contradictions, then, that characterized the suffrage movement in the twentieth century emerged repeatedly in the silent films. Conservative ideas of female superiority, upper-class benevolence, and racial issues surfaced alongside demands for wider roles for women, the dismantling of political machines, and attention to the needs of the working classes. The image of men in the movement's films fluctuated between one of villainous tyrants and weak-willed, insensitive "heroes" who needed women to elevate them. The suffragists' films both lectured male audiences of their "inferior" moral status, and catered to male egos with attractive actresses. According to the films, men needed women to care for them—and the sharp-witted, beautiful suffragists could do the job best. Thought the movement bowed to the expectations of movie audiences with attractive heroines, racist implications, and fairy-tale romance, an angry undercurrent rumbled beneath their cinematic gestures of conciliation. The frustrations and resentments that accumulated against a male power structure during the long suffrage struggle rippled through the movement's films.

Several later commercial melodramas continued the appeal for votes for women with support of the suffragists' long persistent efforts for political equality. *The Woman in Politics* (Thanhouser, 1916), *One Law for Both* (Abramson, 1917), and Maurice Tourneur's spectacular *Woman* (1918) raised issues surrounding the political and economic inequality of women. It is perhaps not surprising, however, that the film debate over suffragism ended in 1919 with a comedy that reflected ambivalance over women's changing roles, and set the comic episodes in the context of the jazz age.

Experimental Marriage (Select Pictures) told a different story about independent women. Starring Constance Talmadge, this comedy featured a newly married couple who lived together only on weekends, since the wife's suffrage work demanded her full attention during the week. Marriage and a political career belonged in two separate worlds in *Experimental Marriage.* Described by one reviewer as a "thoroughly modern young woman of lovable disposition," this flighty heroine finally sacrificed her work for a traditional marriage.[75] McCormick's ethereal "Goddess of Suffrage" in *Your Girl and Mine* had exchanged her white robe for a flapper's skirt, and surrendered her sage advice to the giddy laughter of Constance Talmadge.

Thus the early comic themes of antisuffrage parodies survived World War I in altered form. If independent women were not members of a strange third sex, they were indecisive, silly creatures who needed the love and guidance of a patient man. On the screen world of 1919, when woman suffrage was imminent, a comic suffragist could be attractive and "lovable," as, indeed, was Constance Talmadge. *Experimental Marriage,* however, indicated that the country would defuse the new political role of women by attaching an image of helplessness and irrationality to these independent women. This last comedy made the final film statement on suffragism: America could tolerate "liberated" women as long as they hid their strength behind a guise of frailty and indecision. Overt power would remain unacceptable for women in the decades to come.

From the earliest years, the movies capitalized on sexual politics in America. Suffrage comedies and melodramas offered their audiences far more than entertainment when they reflected and then magnified sexual tensions, and theater screens became a battleground for an ideological war that often neglected the real issues of women's suffrage. The suffrage debate set loose sexual apprehensions that extended far beyond the ballot and shook the roots of masculine and feminine identity. A brazen young film industry stepped without hesitation into the midst of sexual and political conflicts for both profit and propaganda. In the process it exposed the insecurities of a nation of moviegoers.

Conclusion

Ushering in the twentieth century, the early cinematic tales of America's problems came to be mythologies for a modern society that looked to the screen for its gods and goddesses rather than to the sky. Movie houses became akin to the nighttime hilltops from which the ancients watched their own "stars" endlessly acting out important dilemmas in human form. Many films told of suffering, greed, and corruption that appeared to spring from a condition as natural as the constellations. They transformed the historical situations of modern industrial society into what seemed like universal struggles—struggles that existed because of human nature. The filmmakers, of course, stole their thunder from social problems that affected ordinary people. Magnified into universal experience, such tales validated anger about those problems while they pacified it. They became tests of the human spirit for both the powerful and the exploited, rather than the special outcomes of a particular economic and political era in history. With the introduction of personal and spiritual triumphs over adversity, historical issues seemed ahistorical, making their change seem far more difficult. Those scenarios played out on movie screens—like the stories told in constellations moving through the sky—immortalized the human condition.

Speaking a powerful new language to the eye and not the ear, the motion pictures explained a confusing, changing world by providing a new mythology. It was a mythology that contradicted many of the traditional concepts of America. Here were no "people of plenty" living in a "virgin land." Rather, the cinematic myth of the nation's inner cities revealed a corrupt underside of the "American Dream," and its characters—the poverty stricken, the disenfranchised, or the greedy—acted out their conflicts in a closed, narrow world. This was an America of injustices and limitations—but with a new abundance of motion pictures to transform those limitations into entertainment.

The silent social problem films vicariously mended the tears in America's cultural fabric at a time when the country underwent rapid change. Although a number of the early silent films jarred the complacency of moviegoers, they ultimately tended to resolve the problems they raised in a way that comforted and reassured, as had *Capital Versus Labor* and *The Governor's Boss*. The melodramas helped to make sense of society in a way that, for the most part, perpetuated inequality and passivity. These early reformist films reconstructed reality for working-class audiences in a way that both legitimated their frustrations and stilled their discontent. They did this in part by allowing superhuman heroes and heroines to fight their battles—or uncontrollable forces to determine their fates. The motion pictures exposed discontent only to exorcise it with a restoration of authority and, sometimes, with the justice that the impeached New York Governor William Sulzer found only in fiction film. Out of a chaotic world, the films created order and established meaning in terms of romance and individualism—much the way the cinema weaves its myth-making magic today.

Some of the desire for social change, then, channeled as it was into entertainment, grew out of a disappointment with the promise that America seemed to offer the immigrants. The innocent "American Adam" had become guilty, as the muckrakers implied, in the turn from simple rural lives to the urban, industrialized milieu of the twentieth century. When motion pictures reflected that guilt, the result was primarily a cinematic palliative, a bromide, for the social discontent that ripped apart the nation's cities. Industrial America created a barrage of "causes"—and an equally large assortment of solutions that the cinema adopted as a new mythology for modern society. In that process, the cinema linked the need for security with unconscious fantasy, with the desire to transcend everyday life.

Thus most of the films failed to offer substantive solutions for America's problems. Instead, they spun fantasy worlds. In these cinematic worlds, many of America's most pressing problems were made to appear endurable. The ideological problems of the era were transformed into fairy tales. If the poor triumphed, as Stephen Crane's Maggie had observed in the stage melodrama, it was through the intervention of fate. Typically, those problems that could not be endured were changed in these cinematic renditions through moderate reform—change that made little real difference in the lives of ordinary men and women.

Even the melodramas made by reformers typically presented their solutions as a way of soothing the nation's ills. Despite the often sweeping changes these reformers and activists called for, the motion pictures they made typically conceded to melodramatic form, embedding their pleas for drastic change within romantic story lines that tended to defuse the political thrust of the films. In so doing, the films proved the worth of the new entertainment as a "respectable" or even useful pastime, and also appeared to underscore the capacity of society to adapt itself to the conflicts that the cinema pointed out.

More importantly, they resurrected very old solutions to very new problems—all in the format of melodrama. With its codes of excess, grand gestures, and archetypes, the melodrama was an ideal vehicle for translating the political controversies of the period into entertaining myths that made inequality or injustice appear to be an eternal dilemma of life rather than a problem artificially made by society. If the problems appeared overwhelming, then the message was that mere ordinary men and women faced a futile struggle when they attempted to gain control over them. The resources offered by Protestantism, with its emphasis on personal redemption and stewardship, became a cinematic formula to cope with the dilemmas accompanying modern-day capitalism. A moment of revelation with its attendant private change might overcome the problems faced by melodramatic victims of urbanization, overcrowding, changing sex roles, or the flood of immigration. It is an emphasis on personal religious conversion that, even today, serves as a panacea for the larger problems of society.

The cinematic myth of the nation's cities spelled out problems in personal terms, linking public problems with private answers. Many of the melodramas suggested that, with passive endurance and faith, fate would intervene to alter the wrongs inflicted on their heroes and heroines. For the most part, self-determination was a fallacy. One's destination lay in the hands of powerful, godlike elites who could best determine the code of society. Even the woman suffragists, apparently on a democratic quest, made films that elevated middle-class women into the "saviors" of the country and implied that educated reformers — the privileged — might best tend to the ills of others. They shored up Americanism with the Protestant notion of stewardship.

According to the melodramas, America was a nation divided into the privileged and the exploited, and its wrongs were rectified not democratically but by a modern noblesse oblige of the powers that be. The elites typically received an "awakening" before they responded with reason and compassion to the problems that they had created. Responsibility for the social problem fell to the single authority, not the "system." Thus the films legitimated inequality and the concentration of power in the hands of a few, maintaining that a single quasi-religious act of redemption might establish a benevolent, paternal order.

Though the entertainment form of the cinema was new, the roots of its message extended deep into America's history. The notion of human depravity and helplessness was as old as the nation's Puritan settlers. The conversion experience undergone by so many of the melodramatic villains was a quasi-Puritan design of granting meaning to life. Life became a tragedy to be survived through faith in powers beyond one's control. Yet the films introduced the more modern concepts of social responsibility and "progress" — hope for the evolution of society rested in the hands of those who had been "enlightened" through an emotional rather than a rational transformation. The solution to America's disorders lay in a curious blend of old-fashioned Protestantism and the relatively new reform Darwinism. The films were another form of the traveling revival shows, providing an emotional appeal for the "uplift" of the individual.

Yet, for the working classes, that cinematic "uplift" involved a reconciliation to one's lot in life. While "celluloid criminaloids" could redeem themselves and thereby alter society, those members of the "submerged" classes typically awaited change from external sources or succumbed to tragic circumstances. The cinema's labor activists found their answers in romance or upper-class benevolence; alcoholic husbands and once-innocent prostitutes proved the endurance of the family by returning to its fold. The women who roamed beyond the boundaries of marriage in countless suffrage satires landed in troubles that only a man could untangle, converting the women to more traditional norms. And, as we have seen, even the most radical suffragists sounded conventional themes in their attempt to challenge the status quo melodramatically. The entry of Progressive political forces into the cinema brought with it middle-class solutions for problems of both working and middle classes.

Part of those solutions lay in self-improvement, and the films offered a lesson in self-help for the ordinary moviegoers. They did so by reaching into ordinary life in those early primitive films. The films celebrated archetypal survivors and persecutors who derived their power from touching the mundane with which audiences could identify — and then spinning off into fantasy reassurances about the endurance of the human spirit. Audiences watched their lives stretched to extraordinary proportions on the screen by heroes and heroines who typically submitted to fate or were rescued in sentimental denouements. Despite the dramatic endings that resolved the wrongs of America and allowed the powerful to exorcise their guilt, the fact that such problems could be shown at all reveals a twofold process at work. That process indicated to the middle classes that film could restore order and support mainstream values even as it pushed for moderate change. At the same time, the films told working-class audiences that their concerns were important enough to be addressed on the movie screen.

As they looked for a secure financial footing for themselves, the early filmmakers unself-consciously created a network of ideologies that soothed public anxieties. The problems they explored were important indications of the preoccupations of American moviegoers. The conflicts portrayed in the films were as important as the solutions. The repetition of the same issues suggests that these were causes of the deepest social anxieties in a period of rapid change. In a sense, the problems endlessly examined in the films represented a continuity of fears, or recurrent nightmares, among dreamers of the "American Dream."

In one sense, the early films are unique to their time, revealing as they do a special set of problems faced by America during the Progressive era—and the conditions peculiar to a cinema in search of a definition of itself. Public figures and organizations like the National Association of Manufacturers, the Women's Political Union, the National Child Labor Committee, or individuals like Governor William Sulzer, Emmeline Pankhurst, or Margaret Sanger, saw a terrific tool for propaganda in the new medium. They blended entertainment and political purposes in the cinema in a way that has not been so openly done since.

But in that early use of entertainment, the cinema also formulated a pattern that remained with motion pictures long after the age of reform had waned. While, in many ways, the pre-World War I period is a special one in film history, in another sense, the process of problem solving that its films reflect is as much with us today, in modified form, as the evolved versions of the period's primitive automobile or airplane. The "vehicle" of the motion picture has changed, but it continues to transport audiences into a realm where the known becomes fantastic and the fantastic becomes the known. Ordinary problems are lifted into universal hopes. Fears and worries over the meaning of both domestic and public problems are endlessly retold in stories that still, as Siegmund Lubin pointed out in 1912, comfort and validate even as they stir conflicts. These productions informed, titillated, provided fantasies, but—most important of all—they ensured a social order by absorbing protest and conflict. Political controversy might sometimes be a means of profit for the cinema, but the most profitable product the cinema sold was fantasy.

Notes

Introduction

1. See Russell Merritt, "Nickelodeon Theaters 1905–1914: Building An Audience for the Movies," in Tino Balio, *The American Film Industry* (Madison: University of Wisconsin Press, 1976), p. 59.

2. Walter M. Fitch, "The Motion Picture Story Considered As A New Literary Form," *Moving Picture World* 6, 19 February 1910, 248.

3. See Richard T. Ely, *Monopolies and Trusts* (New York: Macmillan, 1900) and *The Labor Movement in America* (New York: Macmillan 1905); Thorstein Veblen, *The Theory of the Leisure Class* included in *The Portable Veblen*, ed. by Max Lerner (New York: Viking Press, 1958); and Edward A. Ross, *Sin and Society* (Boston and New York: Houghton Mifflin, 1907).

4. "Moving Pictures and Talking Machines in Political Campaign," *Views and Film Index*, 20 October 1906, 4.

5. "Latest Films of All Makers," *Views and Film Index*, 19 September 1908, 11.

6. More a frame of reference than a united movement in itself, Progressivism was a broad umbrella for causes and personalities almost as diverse as the motion pictures that filled nickelodeon programs. See the analysis of Robert M. Crunden, *Ministers of Reform: The Progressives' Achievement in American Civilizations, 1889–1920* (New York: Basic Books, 1982). Also see Peter G. Filene, "An Obituary for the Progressive Movement," *American Quarterly* 22 (1970): 22–24.

7. For an excellent account of the political and legal climate in which activists such as Sanger worked, see Paul L. Murphy, *World War I and the Origin of Civil Liberties in the United States* (New York: W. W. Norton, 1979).

8. See, for instance, the advice that the reviewer George Blaisdell gave exhibitors concerning labor union films in his review "The Struggle," *Moving Picture World* 21, 22 August 1914, 1009.

9. Fred J. Balshofer and Arthur C. Miller, *One Reel A Week* (Berkeley and Los Angeles: University of California Press, 1967).

10. "Why?" *Moving Picture World* 16, 14 June 1913, 1138.

11. For an early account of censorship of motion pictures, see Ellis Paxon Oberholtzer, *The Morals of the Movies* (Philadelphia: Penn Publishing Company, 1922).

12. For interpretations of the early audiences of the motion picture, and histories of early twentieth century entertainment, see Elizabeth Ewen, *Immigrant Women in the Land of Dollars: Life and Culture on the Lower East Side, 1890-1925* (New York: Monthly Review Press, 1985); Kathy Peiss, *Cheap Amusements: Working Women and Leisure in Turn-of-the-Century New York* (Philadelphia: Temple University Press, 1986); and Roy Rosenzweig, *Eight Hours For What We Will: Workers and Leisure in an Industrial City, 1870-1920* (Cambridge, Mass.: Cambridge University Press, 1983).

13. Lucy France Pierce, "The Nickelodeon," *Views and Film Index,* 24 October 1908, 4.

14. "Moving Pictures Shows in Manhattan," *Views and Film Index,* 9 June 1906, 8.

15. Frederic C. Howe, "What To Do With the Motion Picture Show: Shall It Be Censored?" *The Outlook* 107, 20 June 1914, 412-16.

16. Carl Holliday, "The Motion Picture and the Church," *The Independent* 74, 13 February 1913, 353.

17. Ibid.

18. See Myron Lounsbury, *The Origins of American Film Criticism, 1909-1939* (New York: Arno Press, 1973), for a useful account of the work of early film critics.

19. Louis Reeves Harrison, *Screencraft* (New York: Chalmers Publishing Company, 1916), pp. 34-39.

20. Louis Reeves Harrison, "Wake Up! It's 1912!" *Moving Picture World* 12, 6 January 1912, 21.

21. Quoted in Robert Grau, *The Theatre of Science* (New York: Benjamin Blom, 1914), p. 106.

22. Louis Reeves Harrison, "The Usurer's Grip," *Moving Picture World* 14, 5 October 1912, 25.

23. "Writing the Movies: A New and Well-Paid Business," *New York Times,* 3 August 1913, in Gene Brown, editor, *New York Times Encyclopedia of Film, 1896-1928* (New York: New York Times Books, 1984).

24. "The Crime of Carelessness," *Moving Picture World* 14, 28 December 1912, 1328.

25. "Writing the Movies: A New and Well-Paid Business," *New York Times*, 3 August 1913.

26. "Capital Versus Labor," *Moving Picture World* 6, 2 April 1910, 509.

27. Cited in Burns Mantle and Garrison P. Sherwood, eds., *Best Plays of 1909-1919* (New York: Dodd, Mead and Company, 1945), p. 525.

28. "Sulzer Hero of Weak Play," *New York Times*, 15 April 1914, 13; "The Governor's Boss," *Variety*, 18 June 1915, 17.

29. "Well-Known Authors Act Their Own Plays in 'Movies,' " (February 1914) in Gene Brown, ed., *New York Times Encyclopedia of Film, 1896-1928* (New York: New York Times Books, 1984).

30. See Leon Harris, *Upton Sinclair: American Rebel* (New York: Thomas Y. Crowell, 1975) p. 150.

31. Jane Addams, *The Spirit of Youth and the City Streets* (New York: Macmillan Company, 1909 and 1913), p. 87.

32. Vachel Lindsay, *The Art of the Moving Picture* (New York: Macmillan Company, 1915 and 1922), p. 225.

33. Margaret Munsterberg, *Hugo Munsterberg: His Life and Work* (New York: D. Appleton and Company, 1922), pp. 281-87.

34. Hugo Munsterberg, *The Photoplay* (New York: D. Appleton and Company, 1916), p. 157.

35. Ibid.

36. For an in-depth account of the subsequent rise of the social problem film and how it mediated problems from the Depression Era to the 1950s, see Jim Purdy and Peter Roffman, *The Hollywood Social Problem Film: Madness, Despair, and Politics From the Depression to the Fifties* (Bloomington: Indiana University Press, 1981). Also see Lary May, *Screening Out the Past: The Birth of Mass Culture and the Motion Picture Industry* (New York: Oxford Press, 1980) for a useful analysis of how the motion pictures contributed to the age of consumerism.

37. Lindsay, *The Art of the Moving Picture*, p. 289.

38. "History and the Motion Picture," *Views and Film Index*, 1 December 1906, 1.

1: Celluloid Criminaloids

1. Edward A. Ross, *Sin and Society* (Boston and New York: Houghton Mifflin, 1907).

2. Quoted in Lewis Jacobs, *The Rise of American Film* (New York: Teachers' College Press, 1968), p. 47.

3. For an easily accessible compilation of the Biograph Company's earliest bulletins see Kemp Niver, *Biograph Bulletins, 1896-1908* (Los Angeles: Artisan Press, 1971). See pp. 242 and 300 for *The Subpoena Server*.

4. "New Films," *Views and Film Index*, 16 June 1906, 8.

5. G. E. Walsh, "Moving Pictures for the Multitude," *The Independent* 64, 6 February 1908, 306.

6. Frank Moss, "National Danger from Police Corruption," *North American Review* 173, October 1901, 474.

7. "The Police Problem," *Harper's Weekly* 43, 2 December 1899, 202.

8. Kemp Niver, *Biograph Bulletins 1896-1908* (Los Angeles: Artisan Press, 1971), p. 60.

9. "Casual Comment," *Film Index,* 24 June 1911, 2.

10. D. W. Griffith, "Radio Speech," Griffith Collection, Museum of Modern Art Film Archive, New York.

11. D. W. Griffith, letter to newspaper, dated 3 October 1907, held in D. W. Griffith collection, Museum of Modern Art Film Archive, New York.

12. Frank Norris, *The Octopus* (London, Edinburgh, and New York: Thomas Nelson and Sons, 1901), p. 487. See pp. 565-71 for the incident on which *A Corner in Wheat* is based.

13. Niver, *Biograph Bulletins,* p. 150.

14. Norris, *The Octopus,* p. 576.

15. *New York Dramatic Mirror* 62, 25 December 1909, 15; "A Corner in Wheat," *The Bioscope,* 20 January 1910, 52; "A Corner in Wheat," *Moving Picture World* 5, 25 December 1909, 921, quoted in George C. Pratt, *Spellbound in Darkness* (New York: New York Graphic Society, 1973), pp. 66-81.

16. "The Wheat Corner," *The Outlook* 92, 1 May 1909, 14.

17. "A Corner in Wheat," *The Moving Picture World* 5, 18 December 1909, 921, quoted in Pratt, *Spellbound in Darkness.*

18. Edward J. King, "His Ideal of Power," *Moving Picture Stories,* 2 February 1913, 5.

19. Ross, *Sin and Society,* 10.

20. Ibid.

21. "The Usurer," *Motography* 4, 1 August 1910, 77.

22. Michael Davis, *The Exploitation of Pleasure* (New York: Russell Sage Foundation, 1911), p. 30.

23. Gabriel Kolko, *The Triumph of Conservatism: A Reinterpretation of American History, 1900-1916* (New York: The Free Press, 1963), p. 2.

24. Louis Reeves Harrison, "The Usurer's Grip," *Moving Picture World* 14, 5 October 1912, 25.

25. "Reviews of Notable Films," *Moving Picture World* 10, 18 November 1911, 535.

26. "Facts and Comments," *Moving Picture World* 15, 14 June 1913, 1111.

27. Lincoln Steffens, *The Letters of Lincoln Steffens,* edited by Ella Winter

and Granville Hicks (New York: Harcourt, Brace and Company, 1938), p. 222.

28. See "The Virtue of Rags," *Moving Picture World* 14, 21 December 1912, 1199.

29. E. Boudinot Stockton, "Pictures in the Pulpit," *Moving Picture World* 15, 8 March 1913, 983.

30. See Thorstein Veblen, *The Theory of the Leisure Class,* included in *The Portable Veblen,* edited by Max Lerner (New York: Viking Press, 1958).

31. "Pictures and Politics," *Moving Picture World* 5, 30 October 1909, 597.

32. For synopses or reviews of these films and others on political graft, see Eileen Bowser, *Biograph Bulletins, 1908-1912,* p. 398; *Variety,* 11 May 1915, 19; and *Moving Picture World* 7, 3 September 1910, 521; 16, 5 April 1913, 54; 15, 2 March 1913, 1238; 16, 31 May 1913, 909; 22, 24 October 1914, 496; 16, 5 April 1913, 61; 17, 20 September 1913, 1308; 9, 30 September 1911, 957; 22, 31 October 1914, 659. Also see Selig Flyers, Selig Collection, Margaret Herrick Library, Academy of Motion Picture Arts and Sciences, Los Angeles, California.

33. *New York Dramatic Mirror,* 8 January 1910, 17. Clipping held in Eastman House Film Archive, Rochester, New York.

34. "The Power of the Press," *Moving Picture World,* 8 January 1910, 17. Clipping held in George Eastman House Film Archive, Rochester, New York.

35. Louis Reeves Harrison, "Superior Plays," *Moving Picture World* 9, 30 September 1911, 957.

36. Ibid.

37. "A Dainty Politician," *Moving Picture World* 7, 3 September 1910, 521.

38. "The Judge's Vindication," *Moving Picture World* 16, 5 April 1913, 54.

39. E. Boudinot Stockton, "The Man of the Hour," *Moving Picture World* 22, 31 October 1914, 659.

40. For an account of Brecht's theories of theater and art, see Bertolt Brecht, *The Messingkauf Dialogues,* tr. John Willett (London: Eyre Methuen Ltd, 1965) and Brecht, *Brecht on Theatre,* tr. John Willett (London: Eyre Methuen Ltd, 1964).

2: A Cinema of the Submerged

1. Jacob Riis, *How the Other Half Lives* (New York: Charles Scribner's Sons, 1890), p. 2.

2. "Trade Notes," *Moving Picture World* 1, 13 April 1907, 87.

3. James S. McQuade, "The Submerged," *Moving Picture World* 14, 16 November 1912, 639.

4. Ibid.

5. "Comments on the Films," *Moving Picture World* 17, 30 August 1913, 982.

6. "Independent Picture Stories," *Moving Picture World* 14, 14 December 1912, 1120.

7. Leon Harris, *Upton Sinclair: American Rebel* (New York: Thomas Y. Crowell, 1975), p. 150.

8. "The Jungle," *Variety,* June 26, 1914, in *Variety Film Reviews 1907-1920,* vol I (New York and London: Garland, 1983).

9. Letter to Upton Sinclair, dated January 18, 1915, held in Sinclair Collection, Lilly Library, Bloomington, Ind. Quoted in Harris, *Upton Sinclair: American Rebel,* p. 150.

10. Joseph Medill Patterson, "The Nickelodeons, The Poor Man's Elementary Course in Drama," *The Saturday Evening Post* 180, 23 November 1907, 10–11, 38.

11. For interpretations and histories of the American film industry's cinematic images of the Jew, see Lester Friedman, *Hollywood's Image of the Jew* (New York: Frederick Ungar, 1982) and Patricia Erens, *The Jew in American Cinema* (Bloomington: Indiana University Press, 1984). Also see "Outsiders as Insiders: Jews and the History of American Silent Film," a pamphlet published by the National Center for Jewish Film, written by Tom Gunning. Undated.

12. Theodore Waters, "Out with the Moving Picture Machine," *Cosmopolitan* 40, January 1906, 251–59.

13. See "Mother's Crime," *Variety* 16, June 1908, 11, and "A Mother's Crime," *Views and Film Index,* 9 May 1908, 12; "Courage of Sorts," *Moving Picture World* 9, 15 July 1911, 38.

14. For synopses of these films, see Selig Flyers, Selig Collection, Margaret Herrick Library, Academy of Motion Picture Arts and Sciences. Also see James S. McQuade, "The Redeemed Criminal," *Film Index,* 4 January 1911, 10, and "More Revival Suggestions," *Film Index,* 17 September 1910, 2. Also see James S. McQuade, "In Convict Garb," *Moving Picture World* 17, 30 August 1913, 1371 and *Moving Picture World* 9, 23 September 1911, 906.

15. W. Stephen Bush, "Was Justice Served?" *Moving Picture World* 4, 12 June 1909, 842.

16. W. Stephen Bush, "Crops of Freaks and Follies," *Moving Picture World* 15, 8 March 1913, 973.

17. "The Fight for Right," *Moving Picture World* 17, 16 August 1913, 724.

18. Frederick J. Hoffman, *The Twenties* (New York: The Free Press, 1965), p. 233.

19. Louis Reeves Harrison, "The Governor's Double," *Moving Picture World* 16, 3 May 1913, 905.

20. D. W. Griffith, unfinished autobiography, held in Griffith Collection, Museum of Modern Art Film Archive, New York. For secondary works on D. W. Griffith, see Richard Schickel's biography, *D. W. Griffith: An American Life.* Also see Karl Brown, *Adventures with D. W. Griffith* (New York:

Farrar, Straus, and Giroux, 1973); Robert Henderson, *D. W. Griffith: The Years at Biograph* (New York: Farrar, Straus, and Giroux, 1970); and Henderson, *D. W. Griffith: His Life and Work* (New York: Oxford University Press, 1972); Kemp Niver, *D. W. Griffith: His Biograph Films in Perspective*, edited by Bebe Bergsten (Los Angeles: John D. Roche, Inc. 1974); Edward Wagenknecht and Anthony Slide, *The Films of D. W. Griffith* (New York: Crown Publishers, 1975).

21. D. W. Griffith, "Radio Speech," held in Griffith Collection, Museum of Modern Art Film Archive.

22. Eileen Bowser, *Biograph Bulletins, 1908-1912* (New York: Octagon Books, 1973), p. 37.

23. Ibid.

24. Mrs. D. W. Griffith, *When the Movies Were Young* (New York: E. P. Dutton Books, 1925), p. 31.

25. Griffith, unfinished autobiography.

26. Lillian Gish with Ann Pinchot, *The Movies, Mr. Griffith, and Me* (Englewood Cliffs, N.J.: Prentice-Hall, 1969), p. 76.

27. Niver, *Biograph Bulletins*, p. 295.

28. Edward Mott Wooley, "The $100,000 Salary Man of the Movies," *McClure's Magazine,* September 1913, 109-16. Clipping held in Griffith Collection, Museum of Modern Art.

29. Griffith, unfinished autobiography.

30. Bowser, *Biograph Bulletins, 1908-1912,* p. 201; "Comments on the Films," *Moving Picture World* 6, 18 June 1910, 1948; "A Child of the Ghetto," *Motography* 3, 15 June 1910, 313.

31. Burton Allbee, "What Does the Public Want?" *Moving Picture World* 3, 12 December 1908, 472.

32. "The Nickelodeons," *Variety,* 14 December 1907, p. 33; Jane Elliot Snow, "The Workingman's Theatre," *Moving Picture World* 6, 9 April 1910, 547.

33. William Kitchell, "Common-Sense in the Studio," *Moving Picture World* 8, 24 June 1911, 1425.

34. Ibid. Ironically, Jacob Riis confessed that he had, indeed, "camped out in a graveyard" on occasion as a young immigrant from Sweden who could find no other place to rest. See Jacob Riis, *The Making of an American* (New York: Macmillan Company, 1901 and 1937).

35. Louis Reeves Harrison, "Something New," *Moving Picture World* 12, 6 April 1912, 23.

36. William K. Everson, *The American Silent Film* (New York: Oxford Press, 1978), p. 227.

37. Bowser, *Biograph Bulletins 1908-1912,* p. 452.

38. Elizabeth Hoyt, "A Million Dollars," *Moving Picture Stories,* 24 January 1913, p. 5.

39. J. Berg Eisenstein and Arthur Leeds, *Writing the Photoplay* (Springfield, Mass.: The Home Correspondence School, 1913), p. 293.

40. Ibid.

3: Labor Unionism: Seeds of Discontent

1. David Horsley, "The Power of Public Opinion," unpublished speech, held in Horsley Correspondence, Hollywood Museum Collection, Margaret Herrick Library, Academy of Motion Pictures Arts and Sciences.

2. Letter, David Horsley to Upton Sinclair, dated March 21, 1919, Horsley-Sinclair Correspondence, Hollywood Museum Collection, Margaret Herrick Library.

3. Advertisement, *Motography* 10, 12 July 1913, 7.

4. John Graham Brooks, *American Syndicalism: The I.W.W.* (New York: Macmillan Company, 1913), p. 39.

5. "Pathe 'Strike' Pictures," *Film Index,* 19 November 1910, 29.

6. William Haywood, *Bill Haywood's Book* (New York: International Publishers, 1929).

7. "Nell's Last Deal," *Film Index,* 1 April 1911, 12.

8. E. J. Hudson, "Rags to Riches," *Moving Picture Stories,* 31 January 1913, 1.

9. "The Right to Labor," *Moving Picture World* 4, 15 May 1909, 634.

10. Ibid.

11. "Capital Versus Labor," *Moving Picture World,* 6, 2 April 1910, 509.

12. "Films Discredit Labor Unions," and "Attempts by Manufacturers to Poison People's Minds Meet Opposition," in *The Chicago Socialist,* 29 August 1910, cited in James S. McQuade, "Chicago Letter," *Film Index,* 10 September 1910, 8.

13. Ibid.

14. "Protest Against Strike Pictures," *Nickelodeon* 4, 15 September 1910, 158.

15. *Report of the Proceedings of the 30th Annual Convention of the American Federation of Labor* (Washington, D.C.: Law Reporter Printing, 1910), p. 338.

16. Ibid.

17. Ibid.

18. Ibid.

19. *Report of the Proceedings of the 35th Annual Convention of the American Federation of Labor* (Washington, D.C.: Law Reporter Printing, 1915), p. 309.

20. Frederic C. Howe, "What to Do With the Motion Picture: Should It Be Censored?" *The Outlook* 107, 20 June 1914, 412–16.

21. "Trade Unions Use Motion Pictures," *Motography* 1, 9 March 1909, 80.

22. "Nickelodeon Notes," *Film Index,* 25 July 1908, 7.

23. "Moving Pictures for Labor Unions," *Film Index,* 27 May 1911, 26.

24. Selig Flyer, *The Living Wage,* held in Selig Collection, Margaret Herrick Library, Academy of Motion Picture Arts and Sciences.

25. "The Latest Films," *Film Index,* 5 September 1908, 4.

26. Ibid.

27. "Feature Films," Film Index, 12 September 1908, 4.

28. "Comments on the Films," *Moving Picture World* 7, 23 July 1910, 193.

29. Ibid.

30. Miriam Finn Scott, "The Spirit of the Girl Strikers," *The Outlook* 94, 19 February 1910, 393.

31. "At the Gringo Mine," *Moving Picture World* 9, 22 July 1911, 140.

32. Unpublished speech, "Women's Trade Union League," dated 9 April 1913, held in Ruth Hanna McCormick Papers, Library of Congress.

33. "The Long Strike," *Moving Picture World* 10, 23 December 1911, 989.

34. Selig Flyer, held in Selig Collection, Margaret Herrick Library, Academy of Motion Picture Arts and Sciences.

35. James S. McQuade, "How the Cause Was Won," *Moving Picture World* 16, 7 June 1913, 1009.

36. George Blaisdell, "The Struggle," *Moving Picture World* 21, 22 August 1914, 1009.

37. George Blaisdell, "The Better Man," *Moving Picture World* 21, 22 August 1914, 1085.

38. "Film Reviews," *Variety,* 16 January 1915, 27.

39. "Union Meets," *Film Index,* 22 August 1908, 6.

40. "Slides of the Cherry Mine Disaster," *Motography* 2, 2 December 1909, 189.

41. Alfred Henry Lewis, "Pennsylvania's Hungry Slaves of the Mine," *New York Journal,* June 1897, in M. B. Schnapper, *American Labor* (Washington, D.C.: Public Affairs Press, 1975), p. 263.

42. Ibid.

43. "The Rescue at the Mine," *The Outlook* 93, 4 December 1909, 752.

44. John Spargo, *The Bitter Cry of the Children* (New York: Macmillan Company, 1906).

45. Rheta Childe Dorr, "Twentieth Child," *Hampton's Magazine* 27, January 1912, 793–806; "When Is a Factory Not a Factory?," *Hampton's Magazine* 28, February 1912, 34–39; "Child Who Toils At Home," *Hampton's Magazine* 28, April 1912, 183–88.

46. Mrs. John Van Voorst, *The Cry of the Children* (New York: Moffet Yard and Company, 1908).

47. Edwin Markham, *Children in Bondage* (New York: Hearst's International Library Company, 1914).

48. Ibid., 352.

49. Van Voorst, *Cry of the Children,* 119.

50. Edward A. Ross, *Latter Day Sinners and Saints* (New York: B. S. Huebsch, 1910), p. 62.

51. For an account of the making of *Intolerance* and the reviews received by the film, see George C. Pratt, *Spellbound in Darkness* (New York: New York Graphic Society, 1973), pp. 210–27.

52. Letterhead, Motive Motion Picture Company stationery, held in David Horsley Correspondence, Hollywood Museum Collection, Margaret Herrick Library, Academy of Motion Picture Arts and Sciences.

53. Advertisement clipping held in Horsley Correspondence, Margaret Herrick Library.

54. Letter, David Horsley to B. M. Lyons, dated November 1, 1919, held in Horsley Correspondence, Hollywood Museum Collection, Margaret Herrick Library.

55. Telegram from B. M. Lyons to David Horsley, dated August 19, 1920, held in Horsley Correspondence, Hollywood Museum Collection, Margaret Herrick Library.

4: Sexual Politics: Public Solutions to Private Problems

1. Louis Reeves Harrison, *Screencraft* (New York: Chalmers Publishing Company, 1916), p. 34.

2. G. P. von Harleman and Clarke Irvine, "Women Start Something," *Moving Picture World,* 27 May 1916, 1515.

3. Ibid.

4. See, for reference, William O'Neill, "Divorce in the Progressive Era," in Michael Gordon, *The American Family in Socio-Historical Perspective* (New York: St. Martin's Press, 1978).

5. For a history of prostitution during the Progressive Era, see Ruth Rosen, *The Lost Sisterhood: Prostitution in America, 1900–1918* (Baltimore: Johns Hopkins Press, 1982).

6. "The Fatal Hour," *Moving Picture World* 3, 22 August 1908, 142.

7. Selig Flyer, "Chinatown Slavery," 1909, Selig Collection, Margaret Herrick Library, Academy of Motion Picture Arts and Sciences.

8. Reginald Wright Kauffman, *The House of Bondage* (New York: Macmillan Company, 1910).

9. For a readily available synopsis of *A Traffic in Souls,* see Steven Higgins, "A Traffic in Souls," *Classic Images* #64, July 1979, 24–27.

10. George Blaisdell, "Traffic in Souls," *Moving Picture World* 18, 22 November 1913, 849.

11. "The Traffic in Souls," *The Outlook,* 17 January 1914, 120.

12. Letter to the editor, "The White Slave Films: A Review," *The Outlook,* 14 February 1914, 345.

13. See E. W. and M. M. Robson, *The Film Answers Back* (London: Unwin Brothers, 1939), pp. 93–95.

14. "White Slavery on Film," *New York Times,* 9 December 1913. Reprinted in *The New York Times Film Review* (1970), 8.

15. Ibid.

16. Robson, *The Film Answers Back,* 95.

17. "Traffic In Souls," *Motography* 10, 29 November 1913, 397.

18. "Recruiting Stations of Vice," *Moving Picture World* 6, 5 March 1910, 370.

19. Ibid.

20. Emma Goldman, *The Traffic in Women* (Washington, N.J.: Times Change Press, 1970), p. 20. Also see "Mrs. Pankhurst at Vice Symposium," *New York Times,* 26 November 1913, 8.

21. Editorial, *New York World,* cited in Mark Sullivan, *Our Times,* vol. IV (New York: Charles Scribner's Sons, 1932), p. 133.

22. "Is White Slavery Nothing More Than a Myth?" and "Popular Gullibility and the White Slave Hysteria," *Current Opinion* 55, November 1912, 348, and 56, February 1914, 129.

23. Ibid.

24. Margaret Sanger, *An Autobiography* (New York: W. W. Norton and Company, 1938), p. 171. Also see David Kennedy, *Birth Control in America: The Career of Margaret Sanger* (New Haven: Yale University Press, 1970), for an account of Sanger's experiences in filmmaking. Interestingly, Sanger gives her film only a passing reference in her autobiography. Her biographer, Madeline Gray, makes no mention at all of the film in her book *Margaret Sanger: A Biography of the Champion of Birth Control* (New York: Richard Marek, 1974).

25. See Granville Hicks, *John Reed: The Making of a Revolutionary* (New York: Macmillan, 1936), for an account of Reed's drama.

26. Sanger, *An Autobiography,* 110.

27. "Birth Control," *Variety,* 13 April 1917, 27.

28. Margaret I. McDonald, "Birth Control," *Moving Picture World* 32, 21 April 1917, 451.

29. "Birth Control," *Variety,* 27.

30. "Bars Birth Control Film," *New York Times,* 14 July 1917, 7.

31. Sanger, *An Autobiography,* 229.

32. "Birth Control Coup," *Variety,* 11 May 1917, 32.

33. Ibid.

34. Sanger, *An Autobiography,* 252.

35. "Would Restrain Commissioner Bell," *New York Times,* 10 May 1917, 11.

36. Sanger, *An Autobiography,* 252.

37. See Anthony Slide, *Early Women Film Directors* (Souther Brunswick and New York: A. S. Barnes and Company, 1977) for accounts of Weber's career. Also see Karyn Kay and Gerald Peary, *Women and the Cinema* (New York: E. P. Dutton, 1977), p. 147.

38. "The Smalleys Have a Message to the World," *The Universal Weekly*, undated clipping, held in private collection of Richard Koszarski.

39. "The Smalleys Turn Out Masterpieces," *Moving Picture Weekly*, 18 November 1916, 19.

40. Kay and Peary, *Women and the Cinema*, 148.

41. Retitled *God's Law*, *The People Versus John Doe* was shown to a full house in Pennsylvania's House of Representatives, as the state legislators debated whether to abolish capital punishment. ("Vital Blow Against the Death Penalty," *Moving Picture Weekly*, 28 April 1917, 18-19).

42. Opening title card, *Where Are My Children?*, print held in Library of Congress.

43. There may have existed two films circulating with the plot of *Where Are My Children?*. Weber indicated that, soon after Universal had bought the film, the same plot turned up at another film company. ("Lois Weber Talks Shop," *Moving Picture World* 28, 27 May 1916, 1728.) No records exist, however, of the competing film, and reviews mentioned only Weber's rendition of the story.

44. "Where Are My Children?" *New York Dramatic Mirror*, 22 April 1916.

45. Cited in Universal Studios publicity material for *Where Are My Children?*, held in private collection of Richard Koszarski.

46. Lynde Denig, "Where Are My Children?" *Moving Picture World* 28, 29 April 1916, 818.

47. While no footage from *The Hand That Rocks the Cradle* is known to survive, an original continuity script is held in Richard Koszarski's private collection of early film material.

48. See Lary May, *Screening Out the Past* (New York: Oxford Press, 1981), for an account of the decline of the Victorian sensibility in the cinema and the rise of the modern era.

49. Continuity script of *The Hand That Rocks the Cradle*, held in Koszarski private collection.

50. Weber's opening statement for *The Hand That Rocks the Cradle*, held in Koszarski collection.

51. "The Hand That Rocks the Cradle," *Variety*, 18 April 1917, 12.

52. "Bars Birth Control Film," *New York Times*, 14 July 1917, 7.

53. Edward Weitzel, "The Hand That Rocks the Cradle," *Moving Picture World* 32, 2 June 1917, 1458.

54. Ellis Paxson Oberholtzer, *The Morals of the Movie* (Philadelphia: Penn Publishing Company, 1922), pp. 122-23.

55. See Garth Jowett, *Film: The Democratic Art* (Boston and Toronto: Little, Brown and Company, 1976), pp. 238 and 463–64.

56. See, for instance, William Kitchell, "Common-Sense in the Studio," *Moving Picture World* 8, 24 June 1911, 1425. Also see A. Van Buren Powell, *The Photoplay Synopsis* (Springfield, Mass.: Home Correspondence School, 1919), p. 30.

57. "Father and Drunkard," *Moving Picture World* 2, 11 January 1908, 28. Also see "Father and Drunkenness," in "Latest Films of All Makers," *Views and Film Index,* 4 January 1908, 8.

58. A. Van Buren Powell, *The Photoplay Synopsis* (Springfield, Mass.: Home Correspondence School, 1919), p. 30.

59. Selig Flyer, "The Drunkard's Fate," 1909, Selig Collection, Margaret Herrick Library, Academy of Motion Picture Arts and Sciences.

60. "Power of the Moving Picture Show," *Views and Film Index,* 3 October 1908, 4. Also see "A Moral Issue" and "Replacing Saloons," *Views and Film Index,* 30 May 1908, 3 and 5.

5: Suffragettes on the Screen

1. James S. McQuade, "Your Girl and Mine," *Moving Picture World* 22, 7 November 1914, 764.

2. For accounts of the political and ideological history of woman suffragism in the United States, see Eleanor Flexnor, *Century of Struggle* (New York: Atheneum, 1971) and Aileen Kraditor, *The Ideas of the Woman Suffrage Movement, 1890–1920* (New York: Columbia University Press, 1965).

3. Cited in Rachel Low, *The History of the British Film, 1906–1914* (London: George Allen and Unwin, 1949), p. 151.

4. *National Film Archive Catalog* (London: British Film Institute, 1965), p. 122.

5. Frederick A. Talbot, *Moving Pictures: How They Are Made and Worked* (London: William Heinemann, 1912), p. 279.

6. "Nation-Wide Suffrage Day Draws Near," *The Suffragist* 2, 15 April 1914, 25.

7. Louis Reeves Harrison, "The Comedy of the Future," *Moving Picture World* 8, 4 February 1911, 230.

8. See John Stewart, comp., *Filmarama I: The Formidable Years, 1893–1919* (Metuchen, N.J.: Scarecrow Press, 1975), pp. 48, 242.

9. See for reference, "Stories of the Films," *Moving Picture World* 5, 2 November 1909, 769; 8, 21 January 1911, 151; 5, 23 November 1919, 561; 12, 22 June 1912, 1128.

10. See for reference, "Stories of the Films," *Moving Picture World* 1, 22 June 1907, 252; 2, 2 May 1908, 401; 8, 25 February 1911, 434; and 8, 8 April 1911, 787.

11. J. Berg Esenwein and Arthur Leeds, *Writing the Photoplay* (Springfield, Mass.: The Home Correspondence School, 1913), p. 292.

12. "Stories of the Films," *Moving Picture World* 6, 25 June 1910, 1101.

13. Ann Watkins, "For the Twenty-Two Million," *The Outlook* 101, 4 May 1912, 29.

14. Molly Elliot Seawell, *The Ladies' Battle* (New York: Macmillan Company, 1911), p. 110.

15. Robert Afton Holland, "The Suffragette," *Sewanee Review* 17, July 1909, 282.

16. Michael Wood, *America in the Movies* (New York: Basic Books, 1974).

17. Low, *The History of the British Film, 1906–1914*, 177.

18. "Stories of the Films," *Moving Picture World* 15, 27 January 1913, 1596.

19. "The Suffragists' Latest," *New York Times*, 11 August 1914, 8.

20. Ray Fielding, *The American Newsreel, 1911–1967* (Norman: University of Oklahoma Press, 1972), p. 65.

21. *The Handbook of the National American Woman Suffrage Association and Proceedings of the 43rd Annual Convention* (New York: N.A.W.S.A. Publishers, 1911), pp. 100–101. Cited hereafter as *N.A.W.S.A. Handbook*.

22. "Suffrage Play," *The Suffragist* 1, 20 December 1913, 48.

23. "How the Vote Was Won," *The Suffragist* 2, 21 February 1914, 7.

24. *N.A.W.S.A. Handbook* (1911), 23, 155.

25. Thomas Bedding, "Propagandry and the Picture Show," *Moving Picture World* 8, 18 February 1911, 347.

26. Thomas Bedding, "On the Screen," *Moving Picture World* 8, 4 March 1911, 472.

27. Advertisement, *Moving Picture World* 12, 8 June 1912, 796.

28. "Stories of the Films," *Moving Picture World* 12, 8 June 1912, 962.

29. "Anna Shaw and Jane Addams in Pictures," *Moving Picture World* 12, 19 May 1912, 617.

30. "Pictures at Hull House," *Moving Picture World* 1, 22 June 1907, 262.

31. Jane Addams, *The Spirit of Youth and the City Streets* (New York: Macmillan Company, 1909), p. 87.

32. "Anna Shaw and Jane Addams in Pictures," 617.

33. "Votes for Women," *Moving Picture World*, 12 June 1912, 811.

34. See convention report in *N.A.W.S.A. Handbook* (1912), 19.

35. See convention report in *N.A.W.S.A. Handbook* (1913), 95.

36. See convention report in *N.A.W.S.A. Handbook* (1913), 101.

37. Reverend E. Boudinot Stockton, "The Pictures in the Pulpit," *Moving Picture World* 14, 28 December 1912, 1285.

38. "New Items," *Moving Picture World*, 24 January 1913, 29.

39. W. Stephen Bush, "Eighty Million Women Want—?" *Moving Picture World* 18, 15 November 1913, 741.

40. "What 80 Million Women Want?" *Motography* 10, 29 November 1913, 407.

41. Ibid.

42. Bush, "Eighty Million Women Want—?," 741.

43. "What 80 Million Women Want?," 407.

44. Aileen Kraditor, *The Ideas of the Woman Suffrage Movement 1890-1920* (New York: Columbia University Press, 1965), p. 25.

45. Advertisement, *Moving Picture World* 18, 8 November 1913, 626.

46. "Big Throng Hears Mrs. Pankhurst," *New York Times*, 25 November 1913, 3.

47. *N.A.W.S.A. Handbook* (1913), 20.

48. "Congressional Union Campaign Propaganda Work," *The Suffragist* 2, 10 January 1914, 2.

49. "The Nation-Wide Suffrage Day," *The Suffragist* 2, 18 April 1914, 6.

50. *N.A.W.S.A. Handbook* (1913), 20 and (1914), 45.

51. *N.A.W.S.A. Handbook* (1913), 20.

52. "Prizes for Suffrage Films," *New York Times*, 2 July 1914, 9.

53. Memoir held in the Ruth Hanna McCormick Archives in Library of Congress, Washington, D.C.

54. McQuade, "Your Girl and Mine," 764.

55. See *N.A.W.S.A. Handbook* (1914), 113, 137, 171, 172.

56. James S. McQuade, "Chicago Letter," *Moving Picture World* 21, 26 September 1914, 1782.

57. "Film for Suffrage Fight," *New York Times*, 4 October 1917, VIII:4.

58. McQuade, "Your Girl and Mine," 764.

59. Original synopsis of *Your Girl and Mine*, held in Ruth Hanna McCormick Archives, Library of Congress.

60. Vachel Lindsay, *The Art of the Moving Picture* (New York: Macmillan Company, 1915 and 1922), pp. 230–31.

61. "Has Initial Showing," *Motography* 12, 31 October 1914, 589.

62. William Henry, "Cleo the Craftswoman," *Photoplay* 9, January 1916, 109.

63. "Doings at Los Angeles," *Moving Picture World* 16, 14 June 1913, 1141.

64. "Suffrage Play on Road," *New York Times*, 21 December 1913, 21.

65. McQuade, "Your Girl and Mine," 764.

66. "Film for Suffrage Fight," *New York Times*, 4.

67. Ida Husted Harper, ed., *History of Woman Suffrage*, V (New York: J. J. Little and Ives, 1922), p. 425.

68. *N.A.W.S.A. Handbook* (1915), 17.

69. Catherine Lyle Cleverdon, *The Woman Suffrage Movement in Canada* (Toronto: University of Toronto Press, 1950), p. 223.

70. Clipping held in Ruth Hanna McCormick Archives, Library of Congress.

71. "The Election Campaign," *The Suffragist* 4, 21 October 1916, 4.

72. "Movies to Help Suffrage," *New York Times,* 9 November 1914, 6.

73. Ibid.

74. "Movies to Teach Women to Vote," *New York Times,* 22 January 1914, 3.

75. Hanford C. Judson, "Experimental Marriage," *Moving Picture World* 40, 5 April 1919, 123.

Select Filmography

The Agitator. American Films 1912.
The Anarchists. Lubin 1907.
At the Gringo Mine. Melies 1911.
The Awakening of John Bond. Edison 1911. Held in Motion Picture Paper
    Print Collection, Library of Congress.

Bedelia and the Suffragette. Reliance 1912.
The Better Man. Famous Players 1914.
Birth Control (or The New World). Sanger 1917.
The Birth of a Nation. Griffith 1915. Held in Motion Picture Collection,
    Library of Congress.
The Blacksmiths' Strike. Pathe 1907.
Bread upon the Water. Vitagraph 1912.
A Busy Day, or A Militant Suffragette. Keystone 1914.

Calino Marries a Suffragette. Gaumont 1912.
Capital Versus Labor. Vitagraph 1910.
A Child of the Ghetto. Biograph 1910. Held in Motion Picture Paper Print
    Collection, Library of Congress.
The Children of Eve. Edison 1915. Held in the Kleine Collection, Library of
    Congress.
Children of the Ghetto. Fox 1915.
Children of the Tenements. Kalem 1913.
Children Who Labour. Edison, with the National Child Labor Committee,
    1912.
Chinatown Slavery. Selig 1909.

The Coal Heavers. American Mutoscope & Biograph 1904. Held in Motion Picture Paper Print Collection, Library of Congress.

The Commuters. Kleine 1915. Held in the Kleine Collection, Library of Congress.

The Convict's Escape. American Mutoscope and Biograph 1904.

A Convict's Heroism. Gaumont 1909.

A Convict's Child. Vitagraph 1911.

A Convict's Sacrifice. Biograph 1908. Held in Motion Picture Paper Print Collection, Library of Congress.

A Corner in Wheat. Biograph 1909. Held in Motion Picture Paper Print Collection, Library of Congress.

The Courage of the Commonplace. Edison 1917. Held in the Kleine Collection, Library of Congress.

Courage of Sorts. Vitagraph 1911.

The Crime of Carelessness. Edison 1912, with National Association of Manufacturers. Held in National Association of Manufacturers Archives, Delaware.

The Cry of the Children. Thanhouser 1913.

Cupid Versus Women's Rights. Vitagraph 1913.

A Cure for Suffragettes. Biograph 1912. Held in Paul Killiam Collection.

The Curse of Cocaine. Essanay 1909.

The Curse of Drink. Pathe 1909.

The Customary Two Weeks. Edison 1917. Held in the Kleine Collection, Library of Congress.

Cy Whittacker's Ward. Edison 1917. Held in the Kleine Collection, Library of Congress.

A Dainty Politician. Thanhouser 1910.

Damaged Goods. American 1914.

Damaged: No Goods. Sunshine Comedies 1917.

The Day After. Biograph 1909. Held in Motion Picture Paper Print Collection, Library of Congress.

A Day in the Life of a Suffragette. Pathe 1908.

Decoyed. American Mutoscope and Biograph 1904. Held in Motion Picture Paper Print Collection, Library of Congress.

A Determined Woman. Independent Motion Pictures 1910.

The District Attorney's Conscience. Lubin 1915.

Drink's Lure. Biograph 1913.

The Drunkard's Child. Lubin 1909. Held in Motion Picture Paper Print Collection, Library of Congress.

The Drunkard's Fate. Selig 1909.

A Drunkard's Reformation. Biograph 1909. Held in Motion Picture Paper Print Collection, Library of Congress.

Effecting a Cure. Biograph 1910. Held in Motion Picture Paper Print Collection, Library of Congress.

Eighty Million Women Want—?. Unique Film Company, 1913—with the Women's Political Union. Held by Classic Film Exchange.

Escaped from Sing-Sing. Vitagraph 1905.

The Eternal Grind. Famous Players 1916. Held in New York Public Library Film Archives.

Everybody Loves a Fat Man. Edison 1916. Held in the Kleine Collection, Library of Congress.

The Ex-Convict. Porter 1904. Held in Motion Picture Paper Print Collection, Library of Congress.

Ex-Con #900. Edison 1910.

The Ex-Convict. Edison 1904. Held in Motion Picture Paper Print Collection, Library of Congress.

The Ex-Convict. Selig 1913.

Experimental Marriage. Select 1919.

Exposed by the Dictograph. Selig 1912.

The Fatal Hour. American Mutoscope and Biograph, 1908.

Father and Drunkard. Pathe 1908.

Fatherhood and Drunkenness. Pathe 1909.

The Fight for Freedom. Biograph 1908.

The Fight for Right. Reliance 1913—in collaboration with the National Committee on Prison Labor.

The Final Settlement. Biograph 1910. Held in Motion Picture Paper Print Collection, Library of Congress.

For His Son. Biograph 1912. Held in Paul Killiam Collection, New York.

For the Cause of Suffrage. Melies 1909.

Franchise Parade. Edison 1915. Held in the Kleine Collection, Library of Congress.

The Fugitives. Biograph 1910. Held in George Eastman House Archives, Rochester, New York.

The Gangster and the Girl. Kaybee 1914. Held in George Eastman House Archives, Rochester, New York.

The General Strike. Gaumont 1911.

The Girl Strike Leader. Thanhouser 1913.

The Governor's Boss (or THE GOVERNOR'S DECISION). Universal 1916.

The Governor's Double. Patheplay 1913.

The Governor's Ghost. Ramo 1914.

The Grafter. Selig 1907.

The Great Mine Disaster. Eclectic 1914.

Greater Wealth. Selig 1913.

The Hand That Rocks the Cradle. Universal 1917.
The Helping Hand. American Mutoscope and Biograph 1908.
The Henpecked Husband. Biograph 1905.
Her Big Story. American 1913.
A Hero among Men. Lubin 1913.
His Chance to Make Good. Selig 1912.
His Ideal of Power. Powers Films 1913.
The Honor of the Slums. Vitagraph 1909.
Hop, the Devil's Brew. Universal 1916.
How Callahan Cleaned Up Little Hell. Selig 1915.
How the Cause Was Won. Selig 1912.
How They Got the Vote. Edison 1913.
How They Rob Men in Chicago (or HOW THEY WELCOME STRANGERS IN CHICAGO. Biograph 1902. Held in Motion Picture Paper Print Collection, Library of Congress.
How They Work in Cinema. Eclair 1911.
Hypocrisy. Fox 1916.

The Idler. Vitagraph 1913. Held in George Eastman House Archives, Rochester, New York.
In Convict Garb. Essanay 1913.
The Inside of the White Slave Traffic. Samuel London 1913.
Intolerance. Griffith 1916. Held in Motion Picture Collection, Library of Congress.

The Judge's Vindication. Reliance, 1913.
The Jungle. All Star Motion Pictures, 1913.

The Kleptomaniac. Porter 1906. Held in Motion Picture Paper Print Collection, Library of Congress.

The Lady Barber. G. A. S. Films, Great Britain 1898.
A Legal Hold-Up. Biograph 1902. Held in Motion Picture Paper Print Collection, Library of Congress.
A Little Child. Biograph 1911.
The Living Wage. Selig, 1914.
The Long Strike. Essanay, 1911.
Look Not upon the Wine. Biograph 1913.

Makers and Spenders. Reliance Films. Held in Motion Picture Paper Print Collection, Library of Congress.
The Man of the Hour. World Films, 1913.

A Man's a Man. Solax 1912. Held in George Eastman House Archives, Rochester, New York.

The Message of the Violin. Biograph 1910. Held in Paul Killiam Collection, New York.

The Mill Girl: A Story of Factory Life. Vitagraph 1907. Held in Museum of Modern Art Film Archives, New York City.

A Million Dollars. Solax 1913.

The Miner's Destiny. Pathe 1913.

Mother's Crime. Vitagraph 1908.

The Musketeers of Pig Alley. Biograph 1912. Held in Motion Picture Paper Print Collection, Library of Congress.

Nell's Last Deal. Edison 1911.

The Nihilist. Trans-Atlantic Features 1913. Held in George Eastman House Archives, Rochester, New York.

Oh! You Suffragette! American 1911.

On the Minute. Selig 1914.

One Is Business, the Other Crime. Biograph 1912. Held in Motion Picture Paper Print Collection, Library of Congress.

One Kind of Wireless. Edison, 1917. Held in the Kleine Collection, Library of Congress.

One Law for Both. Ivan Films 1917.

The Other Half. Thanhouser, in collaboration with the New York Association for Improving the Conditions of the Poor, 1912.

An Outlaw's Sacrifice. Essanay 1910.

The People Versus John Doe. Weber 1916.

Pillars of Society. Thanhouser 1911. Held in George Eastman House Archives, Rochester, New York.

The Politicians. Kleine-Edison Features 1915. Held in the Kleine Collection, Library of Congress.

The Power of Labor. Selig 1908.

The Power of the Press. Vitagraph 1909. Held in George Eastman House Archives, Rochester, New York.

The Prisoner's Escape. Gaumont 1907.

Rags to Riches. Rex Films 1913.

The Reform Candidate. Edison 1911.

The Reformers; or, the Lost Art of Minding One's Own Business. Biograph 1913.

The Right to Labor. Lubin 1909.
The Riot. Nestor 1913

The Scales of Justice. Selig 1913.
Self-Convicted. Lubin 1913.
Slavery of Children. Italiana Cines 1907.
The Settlement Workers. Selig 1909.
The Song of the Shirt. Biograph 1908. Held in Motion Picture Paper Print Collection, Library of Congress.
A Strange Meeting. Held in Motion Picture Paper Print Collection, Library of Congress.
The Strike at Coaldale. Eclair 1914.
The Strike at the Mines. Edison 1911.
The Strike Leader. Reliance 1913.
The Strikers. Apex 1914.
The Strikers. Pathe 1909.
The Stronger Sex. Lubin 1910.
The Struggle. Kalem 1913.
The Submerged. Essanay Films 1912.
The Subpoena Server. Biograph 1906.
The Sufferin' Baby. Edison 1915. Held in the Kleine Collection, Library of Congress.
Suffrage and the Man. Eclair, 1912 with the Women's Political Union.
Suffrage Parade. Edison 1912. Held in the Kleine Collection, Library of Congress.
The Suffragette, or Trials of a Tenderfoot. Selig 1913.
A Suffragette in Spite of Himself. Edison 1912.
The Suffragette Minstrels. Biograph 1913. Held in Museum of Modern Art Film Archives, New York.
The Suffragette Tames the Bandit. Frontier 1913.
Suffragettes. Pathe 1913. Held in the Musée d'Orsay, Paris.
Suffragettes Again. Pathe 1913.
The Suffragettes' Revenge. Gaumont 1914.
The Suffragette Sheriff. Kalem 1912.
Suffragist Pageant and Tableau. Colonial Films 1913.

Ten Nights in a Barroom. American Mutoscope and Biograph 1903. Held in Motion Picture Paper Print Collection, Library of Congress.
Tenderloin Tragedy. Biograph 1907. Held in Motion Picture Paper Print Collection, Library of Congress.

'Tis an Ill Wind. Biograph 1909. Held in Motion Picture Paper Print Collection, Library of Congress.

To Save Her Soul. Biograph 1909. Held in Motion Picture Paper Print Collection, Library of Congress.

A Traffic in Souls. Universal 1913. Held in Motion Picture Collection, Library of Congress.

Trial Marriages. Biograph 1907.

A Trap for Santa Claus. Biograph 1909. Held in Motion Picture Paper Print Collection, Library of Congress.

The Two Sides. Biograph 1911.

The Union Workers Spoil the Food. Gaumont 1907.

The Unwritten Law. Lubin 1907. Held in George Eastman House Archives, Rochester, New York.

The Usurer. Biograph 1910. Held in Motion Picture Paper Print Collection, Library of Congress.

The Usurer's Grip. Edison 1912.

The Victims of Alcohol. Pathe 1911. Held in Film Studies Center, Museum of Modern Art, New York.

The Virtue of Rags. Essanay 1912.

The Voice of the Violin. American Mutoscope and Biograph 1909. Held in Motion Picture Paper Print Collection, Library of Congress.

Votes for Women. Reliance 1912—with the National American Women Suffrage Association.

Was He a Suffragette? Republic 1912.

Was Justice Served? Biograph 1909. Held in Motion Picture Paper Print Collection, Library of Congress.

The Weaker Mind. Lubin 1913.

Westinghouse Works. American Mutoscope and Biograph 1904. Held in Motion Picture Paper Print Collection, Library of Congress and the Museum of Modern Art, New York.

What Drink Did. Biograph 1909. Held in Motion Picture Paper Print Collection, Library of Congress.

When Women Win. Lubin 1909.

When Women Vote. Lubin 1907.

Where Are My Children? Universal 1916. Held in the Kleine Collection, Library of Congress.

While John Bolt Slept. Edison 1913.

The White Slave. Miles Brothers 1907.

Who's Boss of the House? Lubin 1909.

Why? Eclair 1913.
Why Mr. Nation Wants a Divorce. Edison 1902.
Wifey Away, Hubby at Play. Lubin 1909.
Will It Ever Come to This? Lubin 1911.
Woman. Tourneur Productions 1918.
The Woman in Politics. Thanhouser 1916.
The Women Who Knew. Reliance 1913.
A Woman's Sacrifice. Tom Green 1906. Held in George Eastman House Archives, Rochester, New York.
The Workman's Lesson. Edison 1913. Held in National Association of Manufacturers Archives.
The Wrath of a Jealous Wife. Biograph 1903.

Your Girl and Mine. World Film Company 1914.

Bibliographical Essay

The most valuable sources of information for the writing of this book, of course, are the early motion pictures themselves. But piecing together the origins of the early social problem film in America is a task made difficult by a formidable obstacle: the disappearance of much of that footage. Since many of the films simply no longer exist, I was forced to rely frequently on original archival material. The very early film trade journals such as *Moving Picture World, Motography,* and *Views and Film Index* are indispensable sources of information on the films. Their reviews, advertisements, and film synopses provide invaluable insights into the content of the films as well as the critical receptions they were given. The original film bulletins, released by the early companies to promote the films, still exist in motion picture archives. In fairly recent historiography, there have been attempts to collect the original film-related material in accessible books. For instance, Kemp Niver and Eileen Bowser have collected the bulletins issued by the Biograph Company from 1896 to 1912 in the two-volume *Biograph Bulletins, 1896–1908* and *Biograph Bulletins, 1908–1912.* In addition, the New York Times Books has issued a compendium titled *New York Times Encyclopedia of Film, 1896–1928,* edited by Gene Brown. On microfilm, *Motion Picture Catalogs by American Producers and Distributers,* 1894–1908, has been made available for film scholars in an accessible form.

While the existence of such valuable editions and microfilm has facilitated the research for this project, the film holdings of numerous archives provided a variety of materials for this study. Below are listings of my sources and the archives which provided resources for this study. The films I screened are those for which the archive is listed in the filmography.

I. ARCHIVAL SOURCES: FILM AND MANUSCRIPT COLLECTIONS

1. Motion Picture Archives, Library of Congress, Washington, D.C.
2. The New York Public Library, New York, New York.
3. The Margaret Herrick Library of the Motion Picture Academy of Arts and Sciences, Los Angeles, California.
4. George Eastman House Archives, Rochester, New York.
5. Paul Killiam Collection, New York City.
6. Museum of Modern Art, New York City.
7. Pacific Film Archives, Berkeley, California.
8. National Association of Manufacturers, Delaware.

II. PRINTED PRIMARY SOURCES

Progressive Era Books:

Addams, Jane. *The Spirit of Youth and the City Streets.* New York: Macmillan Company, 1909 and 1913.

Brooks, John Graham. *American Syndicalism: The I.W.W.* New York: Macmillan Company, 1913.

Davis, Michael. *The Exploitation of Pleasure.* New York: Russell Sage Foundation, 1911.

Eisenstein, J. Berg, and Arthur Leeds, *Writing the Photoplay.* Springfield, Mass.: The Home Correspondence School, 1913.

Ely, Richard T. *Monopolies and Trusts.* New York: Macmillan, 1900.

Goldman, Emma. *The Traffic in Women.* Washington, N.J.: Times Change Press, 1970.

Grau, Robert. *The Theatre of Science.* New York: Benjamin Blom, 1914.

Handbook of the National American Handbook of the National American Woman Suffrage Association and Proceedings of the Annual Conventions. New York: N.A.W.S.A. Publishers, 1911, 1912, 1913, 1914, 1915.

Harper, Ida Husted, ed. *The History of Woman Suffrage.* Vol. 5. New York: J. J. Little and Ives, 1922.

Harrison, Louis Reeves. *Screencraft.* New York: Chalmers Publishing Company, 1916.

Haywood, William. *Bill Haywood's Book.* New York: International Publishers, 1929.

Kauffman, Reginald Wright. *The House of Bondage.* New York: Macmillan Company, 1910.

Lindsay, Vachel. *The Art of the Moving Picture.* New York: Macmillan Company, 1915.

Markham, Edwin. *Children in Bondage.* New York: Hearst's International Library Company, 1914.

Munsterberg, Hugo. *The Photoplay.* New York: D. Appleton and Company, 1916.

Munsterberg, Margaret. *Hugo Munsterberg: His Life and Work.* New York: D. Appleton and Company, 1922.

Norris, Frank. *The Octopus.* New York: P. F. Collier and Son, 1901.

Oberholtzer, Ellis Paxon. *The Morals of the Movie.* Philadelphia: Penn Publishing Company, 1922.

Powell, A. Van Buren. *The Photoplay Synopsis.* Springfield, Mass.: Home Correspondence School, 1919.

Report of the Proceedings of the Annual Conventions of the American Federation of Labor. Washington, D.C.: Law Reporter Printing, 1910 and 1915.

Riis, Jacob. How the Other Half Lives. New York: Charles Scribner's Sons, 1890.

———. *The Making of an American.* New York: Macmillan Company, 1901 and 1937.

———. *The Labor Movement in America.* New York: Macmillan, 1905.

Ross, Edward A. *Sin and Society.* Boston and New York: Houghton Mifflin: 1907.

———. *Latter Day Sinners and Saints.* New York: B. S. Huebsch, 1910.

Seawell, Molly Elliot. *The Ladies' Battle.* New York: Macmillan Company, 1911.

Spargo, John. *The Bitter Cry of the Children.* New York: Macmillan Company, 1906.

Talbot, Frederick A. *Moving Pictures: How They Are Made and Worked.* London: William Heinemann, 1912.

Van Voorst, Mrs. John. *The Cry of the Children.* New York: Moffet Yard and Company, 1908.

Veblen, Thorstein. *The Theory of the Leisure Class.* New York: Macmillan, 1899.

Progressive Era Articles and Periodicals:

Moving Picture World
Motography
Variety
Views and Film Index
The Outlook
The Independent
The New York Times

Contemporary Books:

Balio, Tino, ed. *The American Film Industry.* Madison: University of Wisconsin Press, 1976.

Barnes, John. *The Beginnings of the Cinema in England.* New York: Barnes and Noble, 1976.

Bordwell, David, Janet Staiger, and Kristin Thompson. *The Classic American Cinema: Film Style and Mode of Production to 1960.* New York: Columbia University Press, 1985.

Bowser, Eileen. *Biograph Bulletins, 1908–1912.* New York: Octagon Books, 1973.

Brecht, Bertolt. *The Messingkauf Dialogues,* tr. John Willett. London: Eyre Methuen Ltd., 1965.

——. *Brecht on Theatre,* tr. John Willett. London: Eyre Methuen Ltd., 1964.

Brown, Gene, ed. *New York Times Encyclopedia of Film, 1896–1928.* New York: New York Times Books, 1984.

Brown, Karl. *Adventures with D. W. Griffith.* New York: Farrar, Straus, and Giroux, 1973.

Brownlow, Kevin. *The Parade's Gone By . . . .* New York: Knopf, 1969.

Cleverdon, Catherine Lyle. *The Woman Suffrage Movement in Canada.* Toronto: University of Toronto Press, 1950.

Crunden, Robert M. *Ministers of Reform: The Progressives' Achievement in American Civilizations, 1889–1920.* New York: Basic Books, 1982.

Erens, Patricia. *The Jew in American Cinema.* Bloomington: Indiana University Press, 1984.

Everson, Willliam K. *The American Silent Film.* New York: Oxford University Press, 1978.

Fell, John, ed. *Film Before Griffith.* Berkeley and Los Angeles: University of California Press, 1983.

Fielding, Ray. *The American Newsreel, 1911–1967.* Norman: University of Oklahoma Press, 1972.

Flexnor, Eleanor. *Century of Struggle.* New York: Atheneum, 1971.

Forty Years of Film History, 1895–1935: Notes on the Films. London: British Film Industry, undated.

Friedman, Lester D. *Hollywood's Image of the Jew.* New York: Frederick Ungar, 1982.

Gifford, Denis. *The British Film Catalogue, 1895–1970.* Newton Abbot, U.K.: David and Charles, 1973.

Gordon, Michael. *The American Family in Socio-Historical Perspective.* New York: St. Martin's Press, 1978.

Gunning, Tom. *D. W. Griffith and the Narrator-System: Narrative Structure and Industry Organization in Biograph Films, 1891–1919.* Unpublished Ph.D. dissertation, New York University, 1986.

Hampton, Benjamin. *A History of the Movies.* New York: Dover, 1970. Reprinted from 1931.

Henderson, Brian. *D. W. Griffith: The Years at Biograph.* New York: Farrar, Straus and Giroux, 1970.

———. *D. W. Griffith: His Life and Work.* New York: Oxford University Press, 1972.

Hendricks, Gordon. *Beginnings of the Biograph.* New York: Arno, 1972.

Hoffman, Frederick J. *The Twenties.* New York: The Free Press, 1965.

Jacobs, Lewis. *The Rise of American Film.* New York: Harcourt, Brace and Company, 1939.

Jowett, Garth. *Film: The Democratic Art.* Boston and Toronto: Little, Brown and Company, 1976.

Kay, Karyn, and Gerald Peary. *Women and the Cinema.* New York: E. P. Dutton, 1977.

Kolko, Gabriel. *The Triumph of Conservatism: A Reinterpretation of American History, 1900-1916.* New York: The Free Press, 1963.

Kraditor, Aileen. *The Ideas of the Woman Suffrage Movement, 1890-1920.* New York: Columbia University Press, 1965.

Lahue, Kalton C. ed., *Motion Picture Pioneer: The Selig Polyscope Company.* South Brunswick, N.J.: A. S. Barnes, 1973.

Lauritzen, Einar, and Gunnar Lundquist, *American Film Index, 1908-1915.* Stockholm: University of Stockholm, 1976.

Lounsbury, Myron. *The Origins of American Film Criticism, 1909-1939.* New York: Arno Press, 1973.

Low, Rachel. *The History of the British Film, 1906-1914,* vol. 2. London: George Allen and Unwin, 1949.

May, Lary. *Screening out the Past: The Birth of Mass Culture and the Motion Picture Industry.* New York: Oxford Press, 1980.

Merritt, Russell. *The Impact of D. W. Griffith's Motion Pictures from 1908 to 1915 on Contemporary American Culture.* Unpublished Ph.D. dissertation, Harvard University, 1970.

Murphy, Paul L. *World War I and the Origin of Civil Liberties in the United States.* New York: W. W. Norton, 1979.

National Film Archive Catalog. London: British Film Institute, 1965.

Niver, Kemp, ed. *Biograph Bulletins, 1896-1908.* Los Angeles: Artisan Press, 1971.

Pratt, George C. *Spellbound in Darkness.* New York: New York Graphic Society, 1973.

Purdy, Jim, and Peter Roffman. *The Hollywood Social Problem Film: Madness, Despair, and Politics from the Depression to the Fifties.* Bloomington: Indiana University Press, 1981.

Ramsaye, Terry. *A Million and One Nights.* New York: Simon and Schuster, 1964. Reprinted from 1926.

Robson, E. W., and M. M. Robson. *The Film Answers Back.* London: Unwin Brothers, 1939.

Rosen, Ruth. *The Lost Sisterhood: Prostitution in America, 1908-1918.* Baltimore: Johns Hopkins Press, 1982.

Schickel, Richard. *D. W. Griffith: An American Life.* New York: Simon and Schuster, 1984.

Schnapper, M. B. *American Labor.* Washington, D.C.: Public Affairs Press, 1975.

Slide, Anthony. *Early American Cinema.* New York: A. S. Barnes, 1970.

——. *Early American Women Film Directors.* Souther Brunswick and New York: A. S. Barnes and Company, 1977.

Stewart, John, ed. *Filmarama I: The Formidable Years, 1893-1919.* Metuchen, N.J.: Scarecrow Press, 1975.

Sullivan, Mark. *Our Times,* vol. IV. New York: Charles Scribner's Sons, 1932.

Wenden, D. J. *The Birth of the Movies.* New York: Dutton, 1975.

Wood, Michael. *America in the Movies.* New York: Basic Books, 1974.

Memoirs, Biographies, and Letters:

Balshofer, Fred J. and Arthur C. Miller. *One Reel A Week.* Berkeley and Los Angeles: University of California Press, 1967.

Gish, Lillian, with Ann Pinchot. *The Movies, Mr. Griffith, and Me.* Englewood Cliffs, N.J.: Prentice-Hall, 1969.

Griffith, Mrs. D. W. *When the Movies Were Young.* New York: E. P. Dutton Books, 1925.

Harris, Leon. *Upton Sinclair: American Rebel.* New York: Thomas Y. Crowell, 1975.

Hicks, Granville. *John Reed: The Making of a Revolutionary.* New York: Macmillan Company, 1936.

Kennedy, David. *Birth Control in America: The Career of Margaret Sanger.* New Haven: Yale University Press, 1970.

Sanger, Margaret. *An Autobiography.* New York: W. W. Norton and Company, 1938.

Steffens, Lincoln. *The Letters of Lincoln Steffens,* eds. Ella Winter and Granville Hicks. New York: Harcourt, Brace and Company, 1938.

Index

Note on the Author

Kay Sloan received her doctorate in American Studies from the University of Texas at Austin and has been Assistant Professor of English at Miami University in Oxford, Ohio, since 1985. She has also been a Fulbright Professor in American Studies at the Université Libre de Bruxelles in Belgium. With William H. Goetzmann, she co-authored *Looking Far North: The Harriman Expedition to Alaska, 1899* (Viking Press, 1982). Among her articles on film are "A Cinema in Search of Itself," *Cineaste*; "Three Hitchcock Heroines: The Domestication of Violence," *New Orleans Review*; and "Sexual Warfare in the Silent Cinema," *American Quarterly*.